SHE'S GONE MOVE ON

Matthew Ball

TABLE OF CONTENTS

INTRODUCTION 3

CHAPTER ONE: MANNING UP...5

CHAPTER TWO: EMOTIONAL MASTERY 27

CHAPTER THREE: TAKING CARE OF YOURSELF 49

CHAPTER FOUR: THE FUTURE YOU.............................73

CHAPTER FIVE: DON'T DIVORCE YOUR KIDS.........91

CHAPTER SIX: WHERE THE RUBBER MEETS THE ROAD......111

ACKNOWLEDGEMENTS

I would like to start with saying a huge thank you to my wife and my rock, Cara. You have put up with me working on this project since 2011. We've had so many conversations and debates around how to approach, write, and structure this book, and without your guidance, wisdom and support, I'm not sure I would have ever finished it. Thank you for being such an inspiration to both myself and our kids. I can't wait to grow old with you and travel the world together. I love you with all my heart.

To my kids, Sadie, Liam, and Ruby. You have all inspired me to get this book finished. You have all played such a large part in keep me accountable and focused on completing this work. You are all growing up to be amazing people. You mean the world to me and I love you so much!

To my mom and dad, Pam and David, and my little sis Caroline. While you are all 4,376 miles away from me, you have constantly sent me your love and support from across the ocean. Being apart from you all sucks, but you are always in my heart. I miss you.

To my dear friend, Erin. Your energy and support have meant the world to me along this journey, and when I asked if you would edit the book, without giving it any thought, you said "absolfreakinglootly". Your friendship has meant so much to me. Thank you for being amazing.

And finally, I'd like to say a big thank you to everyone that I have worked with, past and present! In more ways than you know, you have given me the inspiration, energy, and determination to finish this book. You have trusted me in supporting you during the hardest, darkest times of your life. It has been an honor to serve you.

INTRODUCTION

In your hands right now, you are holding the antidote to your procrastination, resistance and misery for moving on. The strategies that are presented in this book have helped countless men reclaim their strength, their identity, and their passion for life. Some have even said that adopting these strategies has saved their lives!

In 2010, I went through a divorce, and going through the legal and emotional process hit me hard. I fell apart and I hit rock bottom quickly. As my entire world crumbled all around me, I looked everywhere for inspiration and guidance to help me through this emotional journey, and I found nothing that I could relate to. I was looking for something or someone that would help guide me out of those dark places and show me how I could create a new life for myself; one that I was passionate about and motivated to live each and every day!

I remember when I first made the decision to get my shit together. It was an early morning back in mid 2010. After a sleepless night, I had resolved to spend the day locked up in my bedroom. I was an absolute mess, having no motivation or energy to do anything. I was bawling my eyes out under my duvet cover so that my kids could not hear me. Then there was a knock at my door and my 2 babies came in to say good morning, both carrying gifts for me: A colouring of a butterfly and a note saying "I'm so glad to have a funny dad named Matt. You are stroig".

In that moment, something inside of me changed. It's hard to describe or even explain exactly what it was, but in that moment I just cried. I hugged my babies and I cried even more. They were too young to understand what was going on but they held me tight. After they left my room, I got out of bed, looked at myself in the mirror and said to myself "I am strong! I am going to get through this".

The purpose of She's Gone Move On, is to inspire, motivate and guide those that have been impacted by divorce, to move forward and create a life they are passionate about.

You have your whole life ahead of you. Start living it now!

CHAPTER ONE:
MANNING UP

"The moment you take responsibility for everything in your life is the moment you can change anything in your life." —Hal Elrod

If you are truly motivated to move on and create a new future for yourself, you must start taking 100% responsibility for your life. Make the decision right now to start this journey today! After all, your life doesn't belong to anyone else. No matter how your past has shaped your present, it's within your power to take full ownership of where you are now.

There are tremendous and innumerable success stories – both historical and modern day – that describe what happens when we take responsibility for the entirety of our lives. You too have a starting point to redefine and rewrite a new future for yourself; one that is not constrained or dictated by past events or people. When you fully understand this concept, you'll have the strength and power that you've been searching for to finally start moving on with your life. I call this whole process "Manning Up".

The concept is very simple and it may seem easy to apply, but it's not. As you will learn in this chapter, avoiding taking any form of responsibility is an automatic, unconscious condition that most of us have mastered over many years. So just like learning something new, it's going to take practice to recognize when you're not in control of your mind, and ultimately, of your future.

Taking responsibility for my marriage ending was the first thing I had to come to terms with to get my life back on track and point my future in a different direction. Early on, when I started to contemplate why my life sucked, all I had was excuse after excuse, supported by a long list of people and situations that I could point the finger at as the root cause. I blamed everything and everyone for my miserable life, taking absolutely no responsibility for my part in the breakdown of my marriage. And as time went on, I continued to ramp up the blame cycle at warp speed.

However, I was aware of the fact that nothing I was doing was working, as my life wasn't changing; in fact, emotionally it was getting worse day by day. Pointing the finger at other people allowed me to have an "out"; an excuse as to why my life fell apart – which clearly had nothing to do with me – and it was a story I happily shared with everyone I met.

"Manning Up" is simply a way of saying "grow a pair and take ownership of your shit!" If you want a different life with different outcomes, take responsibility for everything you have going on right now, and do something about it. Own it, learn from it, and grow from it! By doing nothing, you create a nightmare not just for yourself, but for those who love and care for you – including your kids. You have this one precious life, so please make a conscious decision to start designing and living it today.

This chapter will highlight why it can be tough to change, and how easy it is to avoid taking responsibility. I will show you how to make that important decision to change; one that motivates and moves you toward a new future. You'll naturally begin to see and experience a new sense of freedom and control, empowering you to design and live the life that you want.

The Big Bang Theory of Change

*"Your life does not get better by chance.
It gets better by change."* —Jim Rohn

So where does your decision to change come from? The decision that will powerfully motivate and pull you toward a new life. Does the decision to finally change your life come from people telling you that you need to change? Does it come from reading an inspirational book? Does it come from finally having enough of living a life you don't want? Or does it come from waiting for other people to change first? Most of us know that we should make some changes in life, but many of us never do. Why?

As Tony Robbins says, "It is in the moments of decision that your destiny is shaped". For many of us, when we look back at a time in our life where we made a definitive decision to change something and then found success, it ultimately came from turning a thought of "I should change…" into a more powerful, meaningful statement of "I must change…". For most people, the mental migration from a should to a must happens when you've truly, finally, and absolutely had enough of whatever you're getting or putting up with that's creating a life you don't want.

When you feel like you "should" change, there's limited power behind it and you'll often end up going around in circles and never making the shift. In fact, it will typically drive behaviors that have more of a damaging effect on your life like procrastination, complaining, empty promises and bitterness. When you make a decision that you "must" change, you see no other option but to find a way to get a different outcome or a different result in life, no matter what might be standing in your way. You can use this decisive choice and powerful state of mind as a launching pad toward a new future – one that you're committed to and in charge of.

The best way to shift from a future of "I should…" to a future of "I must…" is to associate as much pain as you can with NOT changing. When you are truly honest with yourself and look at the life that you'll create by not changing, two clear choices will open up to you:

First Choice: You passively and knowingly accept the current state of your life and all the outcomes.

Second Choice: You refuse to accept how things are, and make a committed decision to start Manning Up, putting you in the driver's seat of changing your own life.

No matter your reason for reading this book, picture what your life and future would look like if nothing changed from what you've got going on right now. To help you see the reality of what that could look like, grab a notebook and write down the immediate answers that come to mind when you read the following questions:

What am I struggling with in life right now?

How is this impacting me physically, emotionally, and mentally?

How is this impacting my relationships, my finances, and my career?

How is this impacting my overall happiness?

How is this impacting how I spend my time?

How is this impacting how I see myself?

If I changed nothing, what would my life look like in 12 months?

Please do this exercise. If you're serious about changing your life, you need to start Manning Up today. If you skipped over this, you'll get nothing out of the book. Please do it for yourself.

When you've finished, take a moment and read everything

you've just written down. Let the reality sink in that this is what your future will look like if nothing changes. Are you okay with that? While it likely won't be the most comfortable story to read, it's one that can give you the energy and motivation to create your new life. Without facing the stark reality of what your worst-case scenario could look like, you'll stay stuck and helpless. When you can muster the strength to stare into the crystal ball of your life one year, or even five years from now, it can serve as the wakeup call you need to build the life you want. This is where the magic of your "I should change…" turns into your "I must change…"

So how do you know when your decision to change truly becomes a must? When most men get there, they talk about having a deep sense of energy, drive, and commitment. Their vocabulary changes. They don't use words to disempower themselves. Many have also described a sense of freedom, one that comes from no longer being emotionally shackled by past events, people, or situations. It may show up differently for you, but one thing I can promise is that deep down in your soul and in your heart you'll know. Something will have shifted and it will feel very different. The fact that you are reading this book shows that you are committed and ready to make that change today.

There are two forces you need to be aware of and overcome to ensure you aren't knocked off the path to living your dream life. The first is your Ego, and the second is the B-Lame game that we all easily fall into playing. If you can learn to recognize and conquer these forces, you will be unstoppable.

Showing Your Ego Who's Boss

Come on, admit it, you have an ego. We all do. And if you think you don't, the voice inside your head telling you that you don't, is in fact, your ego. While we won't get into the science or spiritual world of what the ego is, it's important to understand how it can stop you from moving on.

Your ego exists for many reasons, but in the context of losing love, the ego serves one purpose – protection. It does its best to protect you from feeling hurt, looking bad, showing emotion, and appearing weak to others. Protecting you sounds like a good thing, but in this case, your ego can stop you from truly rebuilding your life.

I'm about to ask you a question and I want you to answer immediately with the first thing that comes to mind:

If your ego had a name, what would it be?

Please don't continue reading until you have your answer. I know, it's a bit of an odd question, but naming that little gremlin that sabotages your life, and giving it some form of an identity outside of you, can do wonders in allowing you to understand who it is, and why it shows up. It will also help you distance yourself from its evil ego powers, giving you back control of your thoughts. In short, giving it a name makes it easier to identify when it rears its ugly head.

My ego's name is John, for the record. John was in overdrive in the early stages of my divorce, and on guard 24/7. When friends or family asked me how I was doing, John would mentally take over and blurt out that I was doing just great, my life was fine, and I didn't need any help. I could handle it. And then, after John was done his kneejerk PR work, I'd return to the internal mental mess I was truly in and barely coping with.

When people offered help, John turned them away and told them I didn't need it. When I first saw a counselor, I had to fill out a form to measure my level of depression and John scribbled in unreasonably positive scores. When people invited me out for social events, I turned up with John as my trusty wingman. I'd hang back while he told everybody how my life was perfect, and he would immediately change the subject anytime anyone mentioned my divorce.

John raved about all the women I was dating and how I was living my newfound best life ever. John even encouraged me to start posting more on social media about how fantastic my life was. But the deep truth was, I was living a lie. I was ignoring the fact that I needed help and support. John, my ego, was blocking anyone and anything from helping me, and most of the time I was totally unaware he was in control.

Here's an example from a guy that came to see me:

Following a recommendation from a concerned family member, Scott finally agreed to speak with me. He'd been separated from his wife for 18 months and while on the outside he appeared to have his life together, his family knew he was suffering. He'd lost weight, was recently fired from his job, was in a lot of debt due to some new spending habits, and he seemed to be avoiding his friends. When I first met Scott, he could have easily fooled me into thinking he was totally fine. But over the following weeks, as a level of trust developed, he started opening up about how he was lost and in desperate need of support and guidance. In his words, "My life is a mess and everything is falling apart. I don't know what to do, where to go or who to ask for help. It's important that people don't see me like this – because it'll destroy my credibility and brand in this town".

Like many men, Scott's ego forced him to display a false sense of "I'm totally okay and life is great!" rather than being honest with himself and seeking the support he needed.

So how does your ego protect you? In short, it tells you what it thinks you need to do or say, and if you're not conscious of it, you automatically do what it tells you to do. It's like it takes over your body and starts controlling your actions. In Scott's case, it told him to act strong and not show any weakness in certain situations. In other cases, it can tell you to act like a total jackass even though you know it's the wrong thing to do.

How do you know when your ego is active? Here are some possible telltale signs that your ego has taken you hostage:

- **You become defensive about everything** – And I mean everything. For example, when the other person you're dealing with is your ex and your marriage or relationship ended badly, no matter what she tries to tell you, you immediately react negatively to it. Everything your ex says comes across as an attempt to prove you wrong, make you look bad, point out something negative about you, and so on. When you get defensive, you cut off all listening skills and only focus on defending yourself and your actions. A great question to ask in situations like this that will put some distance between you and your ego is "what is my ego trying to protect?"

- **You find it hard to accept something** – As an example, many men struggle with moving on, as they cannot or will not accept that their marriage or relationship is over. Why? It's the ego's way of protecting them because if they were to accept the reality of the situation, it would be a major blow to that carefully crafted ego. Most men want the feeling of being in control, and one effective way of doing that is to not accept the reality of what is happening. Keep in mind, the future is only scary if you avoid it!

- **You blame other people** –

  "It's her fault the marriage fell apart."

  "My lawyer sucks. The legal system is unfair."

  "My life is so screwed up because of her."

"I have no money because I had to give it all to her."

Blame becomes your default response to the reason that everything sucks in your life; when in reality, all parties involved could likely argue their version of the story to infinity and beyond. Your crafty ego is protecting you by having you automatically put other people down and blame them for how you're feeling or for the situation you're in. In reality though, your ego is making your suffering continue, because by blaming others, you're putting the onus on them to do something about the issue or problem; by doing this, you give away all your control over changing the outcome. How messed up is that?

- **You are right at all costs** – You feel the need to win an argument or make a point to prove the other person wrong. When you're in this space, you are only focused on one thing – winning. You'll go to extremes to prove the other person wrong, such as spending unreasonable amounts of time arguing, writing an email, or crafting a text. You might even turn to social media and post messages about how you're right and the other person is wrong just to see how many likes and comments you will get back. I get it, winning feels good, and your ego is a master at protecting you from losing or being wrong. But really, what is the point? Do you think you're such a master debater that your ex is just going to suddenly realize "oh, you're totally right; I'm so sorry"? That's unlikely; your ex is probably not going to agree because their ego has kicked in too; busy proving that they're right. It's a crazy ride that no one ever gets off unless you take responsibility for your feelings and actions. Man up and move on! Let them stay on that crazy ride to nowhere while you go and explore more of what life has to offer.

- **You pretend everything is fine** – Let's be honest with one another. Most men don't like asking for help, and if you don't get the support you need, welcome to a miserable and lonely life. I'm not saying you must tell everyone you meet all the behind-the-scenes details of what's going on in your life, but when you find yourself denying help when you know you need it, your ego has gone too far. The suicide rate in divorce is higher for men than women because, in my opinion, women find it easier to seek, ask for and receive help. Our egos can be so destructive that they stops us from seeking the help we need to move on with our lives. When I first went to see my counselor, he told me that the majority of his divorced patients were women. Go figure! A family marriage counselor also told me that when helping couples address issues in the marriage, it's the men that typically cancel last minute, don't show up, show up but don't really participate, and believe that it's the wife that needs all the help.

So how do you deal with your ego when it shows up and takes you hostage? Well, the first thing you need to do is become aware of when it's activated. As soon as you do, you can start consciously detaching yourself from what <insert your ego's name here> is telling you. Eckhart Tolle is a master at explaining this – he says that when you're identifying with your thoughts (as in, you believe them to be true), that's your ego in control. When you are present and aware of your thoughts without attachment or judgement, you create space inside your mind where you can safely observe what your ego is up to, and this puts YOU back in control. Powerful, huh?

Once you're aware of your activated ego and you've created some mental space between you and it, the second thing you need to do is simply explore why it showed up. Ask yourself (not your ego) the following questions:

- What am I feeling?
- Why am I feeling this way?
- What triggered <insert your ego's name here>?
- What is <insert your ego's name here> trying to protect?
- How can I let this go now?

Here's an example that one of my clients, Ian (whose ego's name is "Alex"), shared with me:

- What am I feeling? "I'm angry"
- Why am I feeling this way? "Because it's not fair that my ex has a new boyfriend and I'm single"
- What triggered Alex? "Seeing my ex post on Facebook, informing the world she's found her soul mate"
- What is Alex trying to protect? "Me from feeling alone and sad"
- How can I let this go now? "Acknowledge that she has moved on and unfriend her on Facebook"

These questions will allow you to deepen your understanding of how your ego is trying to protect you and why. You'll be surprised with how much you learn about yourself and why you do what you do. Like that one hot-headed but loyal friend, the ego isn't all bad. It certainly serves a purpose, but it can go too far when it tries to overprotect you and control your actions. With so many emotions firing, it's vital to distance yourself from your ego and get back in the driver's seat.

Please Don't B-Lame

B-Lame is Latin for blame, AKA not your potential awesome, responsible, reality-facing best self (for non-Latin aficionados, that's a joke). Simply put, playing the B-Lame game holds you back from Manning Up and moving on.

Here is something to ponder: when you look back at the moments your life hasn't gone according to plan, have you ever noticed that YOU were always there? One might start to connect the dots and recognize that you may have something to do with how your life turned out – good or bad. You've been busy blaming outward your whole life and never noticed the constant variable in every situation – yes, YOU.

When you blame, you're basically assigning a problem to another person or situation which then becomes the thing that has to change to make your life better before you can move on. Please re-read the last sentence at least five times! The truth is you have absolutely no control over anyone in your life other than yourself. And when you blame others and change nothing in your own life – shocking spoiler alert – nothing will ever change for you.

The only things you can control are your own actions and thoughts. Your shit is your shit, no one else's. And how you choose to look at things shapes everything you see. You can view a divorce, a breakup, or other serious loss of love, as either the end of your life, or the beginning of a different one – and only you can choose that, no one else. This is not blaming; this is you taking control of your thoughts and, ultimately, your life.

So why do we blame? We do it so that we can justify the result or the outcome of a given situation without taking any form of personal responsibility for what happened. It's the easy way out. It's the B-Lame way out. Strangely enough, we learned to do this growing up as kids to avoid undesired consequences, and boy, did we become masters at it.

When you take 100% responsibility for your life, you make a conscious decision to own every single aspect of it, which includes

SHE'S GONE MOVE ON

any outcome or result that has, or will, come your way. When you do this, you eventually begin to see everything that the Universe has given you as a gift. One that helped you become stronger, more successful, loving, connected, passionate, educated, and grateful. This is all part of the journey of Manning Up.

Now, think about an area of your life that isn't working for you. Got one? Does the thought of taking this level of responsibility give you major heartburn? If so, why? Because blaming something or someone other than yourself feels kind of good to a certain degree. When you have someone or something to blame, it takes the pressure off doing anything about it and it gives you a great story so other people don't look at you like a failure. But the outcome of doing this is that you get to stay pissed off, upset, depressed, stuck circling the drain wondering why the whole world is conspiring against you. Get the point? Here is an example:

Colin's wife told him she wanted a divorce. For years, she was bored in the relationship and wanted to enjoy and experience life before it was too late. When she told Colin, he vowed to change his ways and do whatever it took to fix the marriage, however she'd already given him so many chances over the years, she'd had enough. Fast forward three years, Colin's divorce is finalized, he's paying spousal support, and renting a friend's apartment. He's put on about 30 pounds and lost contact with most of his friends. He's been dating but hasn't been able to hold a steady relationship, and most evenings, he's watching TV or playing video games. As Colin put it, "my life sucks". When he came to see me and I asked what was stopping him from moving on and rebuilding his life, can you guess who he blamed? You got it – his ex-wife, Jackie.

"It's all her fault."

"She did this to me."

"She ruined my life."

"It's because of her that I'm living with my buddy and can't afford my own place."

"I have no money because I'm giving it all to her."

"She's never apologized for what she did to me."

"My friends don't want to hang out with me because of things I bet she told them."

Any of this sound familiar? Colin is stuck because he's allowing his story of what happened in the past with his ex to define and control his future. That might sound stupid but it's very real for a lot of men; maybe even you. Colin is so used to blaming his ex that he's become blind to seeing any possibility of how being responsible for the breakdown of his marriage and divorce could help transform his life. And because his ex isn't changing in the way he wants her to, his life will continue to suck.

To get the full value of this book, you need to be 100% real, honest, open, and authentic with yourself. This is your work and no one else's. Nobody will see it, and no one will judge you. In time, you'll have people telling you that you've changed for the better and ask how you did it, but it's up to you to share what you want.

I'd like you to write down some situations in your life that you know, in your heart, you are not taking responsibility for, and that you're blaming on something or someone else. For example:

"I have no money because I'm giving it all to my ex-wife."

"I'm overweight because there's no gym near my house or work."

"I can't find another relationship because who wants to date a divorced guy?"

Really take a hard look at all the areas in your life that aren't working for you. The ones you've been bitching about for months, or maybe even years; write them down. Please keep this list close by; you'll need it shortly.

Blaming also changes how people relate to you. Spending time with people who blame and refuse to take any responsibility for their lives is like hanging out with energy vampires. You feel exhausted after spending time with them. People want to be around others who inspire them, make them feel good, talk about positive things, and don't always focus on the crappy stuff. Many single people who are chronic blamers often find themselves perpetually single, with no friends, or new relationships – go figure.

Blaming ages you too and takes the life energy out of your body. Blaming has a negative impact on your health. When you constantly think about and blame a situation or person, the process of doing so slowly eats away at you because you feel powerless to change. You become addicted to thinking about the negatives versus the positives in your world, and like with anything in life, you get what you focus on. You lie awake at night consumed with thoughts and conversations in your head while losing sleep. You gorge on food for comfort or maybe you forget to eat as the stress kills your appetite. You stop taking care of yourself and don't have the motivation to do anything. What good can come of that?

Now I'd like you to go back to the list you just made and circle one situation in your life that you know in your heart you're not taking responsibility for and are blaming on something or someone else. If you see one that you just don't want to deal with, that's the one to choose.

Ask yourself the following questions in the context of the thing you circled from your list:

- What am I getting out of blaming _____?
- What am I not taking responsibility for, that I could if I chose to?
- If I didn't blame _____ for this, what would be different?
- Who would I be without blaming _____?
- What actions could I take to put this behind me and move on with my life?

Blaming gives away your own power to make changes. When you take responsibility for your life, you put yourself in the driver's seat, allowing you to drive anywhere you want to go.

Time To Man Up

Your life is the way it is because that's what you are creating right now. It has everything to do with how you're looking at the world and the actions you're taking or not taking. The only person that's going to change your life is YOU. So instead of complaining, take responsibility for it and Man Up.

The following four steps to Manning Up are meant to serve as a guide. With practice, this will become a reminder for you every time you come across a challenge. Life will always throw challenges at you, however these are opportunities to grow and move toward a life that deep down inside you want.

Step 1: Break Your State. Trying to deal with challenging situations when we are pissed off or hurt doesn't work well. Most often, we just end up making things worse. To respond effectively, we need to train ourselves to emotionally and physically calm down and shift from our protective and reactive state, to a more effective resourceful state. This is the only way to positively work through any situation.

The next time you find yourself faced with a challenge, first remove yourself from the situation. If you're in a full-blown argument, let the other person know you need some time to cool down before you continue the discussion. Before hitting send on an email or text that has the potential to blow up in your face, delete it or save it in your drafts and then wait 24 hours before you look at it again. If you're sitting at the dinner table and just about to tell the kids what you really think of their mother, ask them how their day was or what they'd like to do after dinner instead. If you find yourself sitting at work or home reminiscing about the past and drifting into negative thoughts, try doing a bit of exercise. Do some jumping jacks or pushups, go for a walk, run up and down some stairs, or blast some great music and start dancing. Exercise releases endorphins into your blood stream which can completely change your mental state, putting you into a more resourceful space to see and deal with things differently.

Now that you've removed yourself physically or mentally from the situation, take some long, deep breaths. While it's dead simple, breathing is a great way to ground yourself in the present moment. It helps sever the faulty wiring mainlining the ego, providing a clearer vantage point to observe your thoughts. Slowly breathe in through your nose for five seconds and then slowly out through your nose for five seconds with your eyes closed. Do this 10 times and notice the difference in how you feel. Once your mood and energy shift, you're ready to move on to the next step.

Step 2: Don't Ignore; Explore. Too often when feelings or problems arise, we just push them aside hoping they'll go away or magically resolve themselves. The trouble is that what you resist will persists in your life. So instead of ignoring your feelings, issues and challenges, explore them. See what you can learn from them.

How do you explore a problem? To help answer this, let's work through an issue right now. Think of an uncomfortable situation you have going on in your life. Once you have something you'd like to explore, grab a notebook and answer the following questions:

1) Describe the situation in as much detail as you can.

2) What specifically about this situation triggers you?

3) What feelings, sounds, memories, actions, etc. does it evoke and why?

4) What could you be doing right now about this problem that would either help resolve it or move it in a positive, forward direction?

5) If this problem were either teaching you or showing you something positive about yourself or your life, what could that be? (Dig deep on this one)

6) How can you look at this problem moving forward so that it positively motivates you to live the life you want to live?

7) What specifically can you be grateful about regarding having this problem?

8) What boundaries could you put in place that would support you in handling this issue in a positive and productive way?

Please re-read what you've put down. How are you feeling about the situation now? Do you have another life situation you'd like to explore that comes to mind? The point of this exercise is to help you truly understand what the problem is, why it happens, what can be done about it, and to help you develop a new relationship with the issue – one that's extremely empowering.

As you build a stronger understanding of why an issue exists, you'll be able to naturally see different ways of handling and resolving it. Now, when I say resolving, it's often the case that issues don't just magically disappear forever, but what replaces them is a new way of looking at and handling those same old issues. You begin to break the tired pattern that's holding you back. The next step is where the magic really happens.

Step 3: Make a Conscious Decision to Own It. This is the point where you Man Up and take 100% responsibility for whatever the issue, problem, or situation is. You now own it. You're no longer blaming anyone or anything and you begin to see it as a gift. It can be very helpful to write out the problem, and then reframe it in a way that gives you momentum to rewrite the future. For example, instead of Colin saying, "Jackie left me for another guy, and it's ruined my life.", he would reframe it as, "Jackie left because I wasn't there for her, and I know I can rebuild my life and be a better partner in future relationships."

When you start reframing problems and challenges, it reprograms your mind so that the next time you think about it, you're able to quickly shift your mood, perspective, energy, and headspace. Just like learning any new skill, the more you practice, the more you can default naturally without thinking. Take the issue you wrote down in the prior step, explore it, and reframe it now so you can own it. Did it shift or change anything? Do you see it differently now?

Step 4: Take Immediate Action. This last step solidifies everything. Once you've calmed down, explored the issue in more detail, and make a conscious decision to truly own it; now is the time to take some form of action to help you move on. Look at what you wrote down for question #4 in Step 2: Don't Ignore, Explore. Pick at least one or two things you could do right now, and do them. For example, in Colin's case, he could begin to write a letter to Jackie (he may never send it) apologizing for his actions in the marriage that led her to leave, or if it's appropriate, he could call her and say sorry. He could also write down all the things that he needs to re-focus on in his life and start assigning some dates by which to get them done.

Once you've walked through these steps, you'll immediately

begin to feel more positive and in control of your future. You'll start feeling like you've Manned Up about your life and everything in it.

The Gift That Keeps on Giving

"If you change the way you look at things, the things you look at start to change." —Wayne Dyer

There's a gift in everything that happens to you in life; however you'll only find it if you look for it. Looking at experiences through the lens of "what's the gift I've been given?" is a powerful way of re-framing negative experiences. When crap hits the fan, we tend to focus on the negative, however looking at it in a different light completely changes the experience. Here's an example:

When Calvin came to see me, he'd just discovered that his wife had been having an affair. In fact, he found out she'd been having affairs for the past three years with four different men. As you can imagine, he was an absolute mess and didn't know what to do. He was so focused on the hurt and deception that he couldn't see the forest for the trees. I asked a simple question to help shift his perspective:

"What is the gift in all of this?"

The question threw him off, so I asked it again.

He said, "I guess the gift is that I know she's not invested in this relationship anymore so at least I know where we stand."

I asked him "Is that a good thing to know?"

He said, "Of course it is."

"So" I asked "What does that give you then?"

Calvin replied "Truth and freedom"

From that point forward, my conversation with Calvin about

moving on with his life was more positive. He knew he still had a steep hill to climb, but the question allowed him to start his journey with a better attitude about his situation and future.

Whatever you're struggling with right now, ask yourself "what is the gift in all of this?" The question will help you shift to more empowering thoughts, helping you accept the reality of your situation and uncover a path to move forward.

Summary

You now know that shifting an "I should" to an "I must" is the key to change. Any "shoulds" in your life are nothing but powerless commitments, ones that you know deep down you'll never do anything about, even though you think and say you will. When something becomes a must, your reason behind doing it is so strong and personal that it turns into a solid commitment. A commitment that you'll spend time and energy on, no matter what; even when you come up against roadblocks.

We discussed how the ego protects you from harm and looking stupid, but it also holds you back from reaching out for help and being 100% honest with yourself and those who love and care for you. It shuts you off from the real world and keeps your emotions, wants, and dreams hidden. Be aware of it, show it who's boss and don't be controlled by it.

B-Lame isn't cool! It's a ridiculous game people play to point the finger at someone or something else. This game loves supporting the ego and together they put up so many defenses that at times, you may feel like the chances of creating an amazing life is impossible – it's not! Make a conscious decision to take responsibility for everything. Look in the mirror and point the finger at the person staring back. This will give you the power and motivation to change what needs to be changed so that you can move on.

Finally, believe that there is a gift in everything that happens to you in your life, while remembering that you will only find that gift if you look for it. By asking yourself what gift this challenge is giving you, I promise it will shine a completely different perspective on what you're going through. Life is full of learning and treasures. You just need to be open to them, have a little bit of humility, and do the work to find them.

CHAPTER TWO:
EMOTIONAL MASTERY

"Your thoughts affect your emotions. Your emotions affect your decisions. Your decisions affect your life." —Unknown

Have you experienced a day where one minute you're feeling great about life and the next, you're spinning out of control? Imagine being in a great mood after leaving a party where you met up with a bunch of friends you haven't seen in a while, and then your ex calls. As soon as you see her name, the argument you had a few days ago pops into your head. You start to feel angry and you're now mentally preparing for a big fight before you even answer her call. Or maybe you're on your way to drop off your kids at your ex's house after spending a great day with them and you feel on top of the world, but out of nowhere you start feeling sick to your stomach imagining what they must be going through seeing their mom and dad separate.

If you're a journal keeper and you reflect back at some of your previous entries, you might notice how some days you went from excited, to motivated, to sad, to angry, to caring, to not caring about anything, to anxious, to nervous, to worried, to stressed and back to happy. There will be days in your life when it feels like you're strapped in an emotional rollercoaster speeding out of control. There will be ups and downs and curve balls whipping your emotions all over the place. On these days, it can be easy to lose all motivation to pick yourself back up and move on. This is why emotional mastery is so important. Being able to control your emotional state instead of allowing it to control you, and gaining an understanding of why you react the way you do, are powerful must-have skills to possess as you start to rebuild and move on with your life.

Stop Believing in Scary Tales

When you dig down to the root of what causes anyone to get emotional, stressed, angry or anxious, it comes down to the story they're telling themselves about a given situation or experience; past, present, or future. And if you consider the following statement to be true – that 'Nothing in life has any meaning apart from the meaning YOU give it', you truly are in control of your emotional state and the lens through which you look at life. To put it another way, the meaning you give to anything that happens to you in life is based on the thought(s) that you assign in that moment to whatever happened, is happening, or is going to happen. I know this concept seems deep and overwhelming at this moment, however please know that once I break this down and you understand it, it will be life changing. Stay with me; this will totally make sense by the end of this chapter. I want you to digest this once more before we move on – 'Nothing in life has any meaning apart from the meaning YOU give it'

Here are a few examples of the types of far-fetched stories that we can create in our minds. Let's say you're out getting groceries and you see your ex with another man, and she appears to be happy. You think to yourself that she looks much happier with him because (and here comes the story, AKA the meaning you're assigning to this experience) she never loved you and she basically lied for your entire relationship about how she cared about you.

Or maybe one evening, on the drive home you start to imagine what happened when your ex met up with her best friend who recently got divorced (and here comes the story, AKA the meaning you're assigning to this experience) and how she probably told your ex to find the nastiest lawyer in town just to screw you over cause it's what she did.

How about this one – last night you got dumped by a girl that you've been seeing for months (and here comes the story, AKA the meaning you're assigning to this experience) and you come to the conclusion that you're totally screwed up and dating is pointless because you're never going to be able to find someone to enjoy life with again.

The point here is that none of the stories you're telling yourself are true, because for the most part you just made them up. It is most likely that the reality of the situation is completely different from the illusion that you have just created, but because they appear totally real to you inside your mind, you act, and are affected as if they are true. This is what causes you to become an emotional mess. Can you start to see how crazy this ride is?

What was the last thing you thought about today that got you all wound up or emotional? It doesn't have to be something big, just something that triggered you to either get fired up, down on yourself, or emotionally drained. What story did you tell yourself about it? Now ask yourself, "is that story really the truth?". Can you see how your thoughts (AKA the story) impacted you?

What you may not realize or understand is that you possess the power to give anything any meaning you want. Just think about that for a moment, you are actually the architect of your thoughts. The cool thing about that is when you change the meaning behind what happened or is happening to you into something more positive and powerful, it gives you a new lens to experience and live life through.

This new lens then allows a new future to come into focus, and that is downright awesome.

It took me a while to become conscious of the fact that I was the root cause of my emotional mess. Most days, I went from highs to lows, sometimes in seconds flat. I would wake up in the morning feeling great, and within a matter of minutes I was upset about something solely because of the thoughts and stories inside my head. I remember one day finishing a great workout at the gym, feeling strong and motivated. As I got to my car, I received a call from our mediator and within seconds I was a shaking nervous wreck, fearing what she was going to say. At the end of each day, I found myself emotionally drained from all the highs and lows I experienced. I literally had no mental space for anything else in my head. My mind was consumed with negative thoughts and pointless conversations. It felt like the world was against me and I couldn't do anything about it. Sound familiar?

If I metaphorically cracked open the head of any guy who talks about how his life sucks, how he feels depressed, lonely, and sad, and look at what's going on inside, he would be emotionally short-circuiting all over the place; not realizing that his faulty wiring is controlling his life and his future. I feel for these guys as I was in that place too. I feel their pain, their anger, and worry. If they could only understand that they are in control of these emotional states they are getting stuck in, it would drastically improve their mental state.

Take Graham's experience for example:

"My ex was supposed to drop the kids off at 5pm. But instead, she showed up half an hour late. It makes me angry every time she does this. She clearly has no respect for my time and only gives a damn about her own life. I have a busy life too."

Graham told me that he flew off the handle when she dropped the kids off that night. However, he later found out that the reason she was late was because she took the kids to a store to buy him a birthday card so they could give it to him on his birthday a few days later. Can you see how the story Graham told himself caused him to react the way he did? How do you think his ex felt when she drove away?

"There is nothing good or bad, but thinking makes it so."
—Shakespeare

It's your thoughts, not your environment that trigger your emotions. How you feel and think about things is what's holding you back. When you realize that you are in control of all of this, your journey to emotional mastery begins. And when you start to master your emotions one day at a time, your whole world begins to change right in front of your eyes.

This may all make sense to you on a logical level, but it really needs to sink in on an emotional and practical level too. Let's take a deeper dive into why we do what we do and how we can change it.

Mr. Fix-It

Most of us men like to understand how things work and how to fix them, so let's look at how we create all the crap inside of our heads. Full disclosure: I'm not a neurologist or a psychiatrist, however, I've read, according to my wife, "way too many" personal development books. I've lost love and come out on the other side, and I've helped countless men do the same. Through all my experience and research, I consistently witness the following pattern:

1) **An event/experience happens to you:** *My wife had an affair with my best friend.*

2) **You make up a meaning for why it happened**: *I'm a failure. She's a bitch. She never loved me. She lied to me. She's*

a fake. She doesn't care. She can never be trusted. She's crazy and needs help. I'm a loser, I'm not good enough.

It's important to point out here, if you have not figured it out already, that the second stage described above becomes the lens through which you now look at life. In the above case, it negatively effects how you see your ex and how you see yourself. I know that this is such a simple thing to understand, but in reality it all happens so quickly and subconsciously that most of us are unaware of what we are doing to ourselves.

The factual event of what happened to you (a breakup, divorce, friends not returning phone calls, etc.) and the meaning you give it are two very different things. Why is it that one man can look at divorce and think to himself "my life is over", yet another can look at divorce and accept it as positively life changing? When losing love is the event, the response to it can be anything of your choosing. Reality will remain reality, but what we believe about it is where the win is. Remember, you are the architect of your thoughts.

So how do you reach emotional mastery? Through a committed daily practice! Over time, you'll become aware of when your emotions are beginning to take over and you'll be able to simply detach yourself from the chaos at play. This is easier said than done and especially hard to do in the beginning, but with practice it will become easier. The goal here is to stop yourself from falling down the emotional rabbit hole before you hit bottom, no matter what's going on in your life. It's catching yourself before you explode into an emotional state – both internally and in the outside world.

Here are three things that you can do to significantly help you out:

Spot the Triggers: A trigger is something or someone that sets you off. If you can learn what sorts of things trigger you, you can be a lot more mindful going into situations before they get out of hand. Being mindful basically means noticing. Things can't happen unconsciously in the dark if you're present to what's going on in your mind.

Buy Some Breathing Room: Taking some deep breaths works exceptionally well when you find yourself boiling up inside. For example, you're in a great mood, you see your ex from a distance and within seconds you recall your latest argument. If you're able to quickly recognize this happening (physical clues like your quickening heartbeat, clenched jaw, etc.), and then take some simple deep breaths, it's amazing what kind of distance you can place between you and that all-encompassing rage. It's the difference between maintaining control and composure, and veering off down a regrettable warpath.

Rise Above: Whenever you stop yourself from going into emotional overload, give yourself a pat on the back and recognize what you've just accomplished. It's no easy task. But the more you do it, the better you get at it. Whatever you're feeling, it's important not to ignore it. Drowning your sorrows or wallowing in denial may be extraordinarily strong urges to overcome. But the more you can identify what you're experiencing versus adopting the emotion, the stronger you become in finding a way through.

You may already be familiar with Elisabeth Kübler-Ross & David Kessler's Five Stages of Grief. If not, here are the five stages:

1. Denial

2. Anger

3. Bargaining

4. Depression

5. Acceptance

The Five Stages of Grief framework is a great resource to help you figure out where you might be at on your own emotional journey. It helps put into context the stages that you might go through when dealing with a divorce. Someone you care about doesn't have to die for you to suffer the stages of grief. Divorce is the loss of a marriage, a union, a partnership, and when you lose that, it can often feel like someone died.

No matter which stage you might be in right now, please know that you are absolutely not going crazy, and there is nothing wrong with you. In fact, thousands of people have gone and will go through the same things you're going through. I know when I was in the midst of my divorce, it felt like I was the only person on this planet who had ever experienced anything like it. While things may show up differently for each person, we essentially all go through the same journey; we just move through the stages at our own pace. The key is to *work through these stages;* know where you're at and have the resources in place to help you finally reach the finish line, known as acceptance.

Here is a breakdown of the Five Stages of Grief through the lens of divorce:

1. Denial: AKA ego territory. The powerful denial capabilities of the average human are astounding. People can be suffering from great pain yet appear fine. Men are particularly prone to denial. Your ego will pull out all the stops to protect you from becoming emotionally overwhelmed, often crafting a bunch of stories for you to believe. While denial can be a useful coping mechanism in the short term, it typically progresses into its unruly cousin – anger. When you're in denial, it's okay to use it to your advantage, but only in small doses. Remember, refusing to face reality keeps you stuck. Nothing can be improved that isn't first acknowledged.

2. Anger: I went in and out of this stage for months. As we discussed in the "Manning Up" chapter, when your world is falling apart, who better to blame for all your problems than your ex? This is the stage when you begin to really hate your ex for what they did or didn't do. You may even find that you're hating yourself for your part in the breakdown of the relationship. You also begin to find fault in anything and everything in your life. Hate and anger that runs rampant are dangerous and poisonous to your energy, health, relationships, and life in general. Many men that I've worked with have lived stuck in this stage for years. As a client once said, "I've lost years of my life that I'll never get back because I was constantly angry at everything".

It may be important to go through this stage to get things out of your system, but it's equally important to play an active role in how you're going through it. When you feel yourself getting upset or angry, try to put some space between you and others around you, and please never get angry around your kids. Don't let the anger control you and cause you to say something that you'll either regret or that will get you into a whole heap of trouble, such as sending that email to your ex blasting them for something that you'll regret down the road, or posting careless rants on social media that could come back and haunt you. Keep track of outlets as you come across them – maybe that kickboxing class wasn't the anger therapy you expected but cleaning your house while listening to loud music did the trick. It's different for everyone but the key is to pay attention and keep trying. Get whatever you need to get out of your system in a healthy way so you can move on. If needed, get a professional to help you deal with this stage.

3. Bargaining: In this stage, you'll try desperately to travel back in time and undo every mistake you've ever made. You'll bargain with whatever higher power you believe in and everyone around you. You will do anything you can just have things back to the way they were. Whatever you're bargaining to gain back is likely better than your current reality, so you'd gladly settle for it. You might get caught up idolizing your ex or what you had together. You might go to desperate measures to get your ex back at all costs, self-esteem and pride be damned. Going into bargaining mode can happen when you're overrun with fear. When I've asked men about why they are so desperate to get back with their exes, they would tell me how much they love them and how they'll change for the better, etc. But when I ask "is it truly what you want?" and give them a day or two to think about it, most come back and say no or that they're not sure. It was the fear of completely losing their ex and the fear of an unknown future that was driving them to bargain to get things back. This can be a stage of extreme turmoil and confusion, however it's important to remember that this too shall pass.

4. Depression: Enter the Netflix-binging, and "I-can't-be-bothered-to-do-anything" zone. After all the heightened emotions of the first three stages, suddenly this stage could plummet you into the depths of depression like you've never known. Everything seems empty and meaningless including taking care of your basic personal hygiene and any basic physical movement. Darkness has the tendency to act as the underlying theme lurking in the background haunting you. This is where your A-Team (which we'll talk about in Chapter 3) needs to be assembled and relied upon heavily, especially the professionals you've signed up for the task. If you find yourself struggling with depression, please turn to those who are qualified to get you through this quicksand stage.

5. Acceptance: Along this bumpy road, you'll get glimpses of acceptance all through your journey; sometimes it may be for only a few seconds. But just when you thought there was no way out, you see the door. This is the light at the end of the tunnel, when suddenly you begin to start seeing the humor and hope in things. You've come through hell and emerge on the other side all the wiser. You see the lessons, even some silver linings and you're grateful you survived because there's still life to live and things you haven't done yet. This doesn't mean life is suddenly a bed of roses. Negative emotions will still pop up, and it's natural to still feel sadness and anger about divorce. But rather than be debilitated by those emotions, you find the will to carry on. You might not love your new reality but you do start to accept it. Depending on how things played out, a part of you may always be grieving – but it no longer stops you from moving forward.

You are Not Your Emotions

We often identify ourselves as an emotion. For example, you might say "I am angry". However, if you think about this for a moment, are YOU actually angry? You may be feeling angry, but YOU are not actually angry. Please re-read that last sentence as I want this to really sink in. There is actually a big difference between the two and when you disidentify with an emotion, it's almost as if you take away its power of controlling you.

The most effective way to do this is by changing the vocabulary you use to describe your emotions, whether it's what you say to yourself out loud, inside your head, in your journal, or to another person. For example, saying "I am sad" can easily be reframed as "I feel sad" or you might even say "oh, there's sadness popping up again". As you read this, can you see and feel the difference between the two? Say them out loud and try it out for yourself.

When you've disconnected from being the emotion to now just feeling the emotion, you can safely explore why it's there – trust me, it showed up for a reason. Try running through the following steps whenever you feel difficult emotions bubble up. It helps to collect your answers in a journal as a way of keeping a sort of emotional reference book to track your progress.

Step 1: Acknowledge what you're feeling by name in order to gain emotional distance. For example, *"Oh hi Sadness, how are you?"* Even though this may all sound odd, it really does work. When I initially started doing this, I imagined the emotion as a colour or an object outside of my body. This helped to distance myself from it.

Step 2: Ask the emotion a few questions and listen. Interrogate it a little:

1. What triggered you?

2. Why did you show up?

3. What are you trying to show me about myself?

It's important that you ask question #3 the way it is noted above. If you were to ask "what are you trying to show me?", the answer might be "I'm trying to show you how much of a loser your ex is". By asking "what are you trying to show me about myself?", it changes the question to focus on YOU, which is who we care about and want to help. Now the response could be "I'm showing you that by not having the conversation with your ex about the kids and what she's telling them, you'll end up regretting doing nothing". Powerful answers and insights can come from doing this exercise.

Step 3: Thank and acknowledge the emotion, then say goodbye to it. This is a critical step in completing the exercise. It shows the emotion that it no longer serves you or requires a place in your mind. You've learned what you can from it and it's time to say goodbye.

Step 4: Now that you've learned why the emotion showed up, you need to take some level of action to address the underlying cause. By taking action, you're taking positive and powerful steps to move on with your life versus running away from the issue. This is massively important. If no action is taken, things remain the same and you stay stuck. You can't change anything without taking action.

The Rings of Fire

Another tool you have in your arsenal is the power to change the meaning of anything you want. We unconsciously assign so many meanings to things in our lives and when they are disempowering, it keeps us stuck. This is a simple exercise that can have a powerful impact on the rest of your life. So, let's get down to it.

Grab your journal and draw three circles horizontally and in line with one another, making sure they are big enough that you can write in them. At the top of the first circle, write "What Happened?" On top of the second, write "What Did I Make it Mean?" And on top of the third circle, write "What Do I Want to Make it Mean?" It should look something like this:

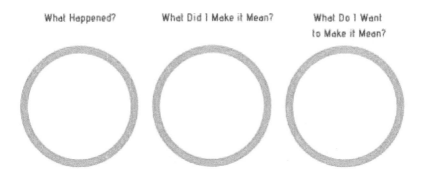

Here is how this works.

Circle 1: What Happened?

Think of a negative event that happened to you in the past. In this circle, write down the facts around what happened and only the facts. Don't associate any emotions with this part. Keep it short and sweet. For example:

"My ex called to say she's been seeing someone for over six months now and wants to introduce him to our kids."

If you associated emotions with the above, it may have looked like this:

"My ex has managed to find some loser who is probably no good for her and now she wants to introduce him to our kids and ruin their lives too."

Circle 2: What did I Make it Mean?

This is where we create our story. Dump all your emotions and feelings into this area. Working with the example above, it might look something like this:

"She clearly didn't care about our marriage, and she's proved that she has no respect for my feelings. She's moved on so quickly that it's proof she didn't give a crap about me. I need to find someone too that I can introduce to my kids so I can show her what it feels like. This guy has money so how can I compete with that? She's creating a nice little family unit and my kids won't want to be around me anymore. I need to find out some dirt on this guy so I can prove to her that she's making a mistake."

Whatever goes into the second circle always provides great insight into what kinds of scary tales we're telling ourselves. It's clear in the example above that this particular story will only lead to a negative outcome where there will be a lack of support and a great deal of resentment between all parties.

Circle 3: What Do I Want to Make It Mean?

This is where the magic happens. It's where you decide to take responsibility and action towards the life you *want* to create. This is where you get to decide a new meaning. An example could look like this:

"I want this to mean that my ex has found happiness and she is in a much better place than she was in our marriage. Our kids will start to see that both of us have moved on while still caring for one another. I will be there to support our children as they go through this transition which will set them up for success when I find a new relationship. I want to show others around me that two people going through a breakdown in their marriage can have a good, decent relationship and not destroy one another."

As you can see the new meaning created in Circle 3 is entirely different from the destruction that is in Circle 2. It's one that speaks to moving forward, empowerment, accountability, and a commitment to living a positive life.

Here is another example of this exercise; in this case we'll go back to Graham and his ex being late dropping the kids off. His Rings of Fire exercise might look like this:

Circle 1: What Happened?

"My ex dropped off the kids at 5:30 p.m., after we had agreed on 5:00 p.m."

Circle 2: What did I Make it Mean?

"She doesn't care about me or even respect my time. The kids are clearly having more fun with her than they do with me."

Circle 3: What Do I Want to Make it Mean?

"My ex was clearly having a fun time with the kids, and she wanted to give them a great experience to get their minds off the divorce. I'm grateful she's so connected to the kids and always puts them first. She is an amazing mom."

The Rings of Fire exercise is a simple exercise that can help you reframe your experiences from the past which in turn will have a powerful impact on the rest of your life.

In Case of Emotions: Emergency Procedure

In life, there are situations like flying on an airplane or boarding a cruise ship where you will be given a set of instructions to follow in the event of an emergency. The reason for doing this is so you don't have to figure out what to do in the actual event of an emergency. If you are going through a hard time and you find yourself on the brink of an emotional melt-down or blow-up while in the middle of a phone call, email, text, meeting or otherwise, follow these instructions below:

Get some distance: If you are physically with another person or talking to them on the phone, say to them "I'm sorry but I need to remove myself from this situation. I need some time to collect my thoughts" and then either leave, walk away, or hang up the phone. If you're by yourself and you just received an email or text, try going for a walk or move into a different room.

Get some oxygen: Once you've got some distance, breathe deeply. Breathe in through your nose slowly for a count of five, then breathe out through your nose slowly for the count of five. Do this for at least five breaths.

Call an A-Team member (this will be covered in Chapter 3): Or find someone qualified to talk to. If that's not an option, write down what's going on in your mind – get it all out of your head and onto the page. If you keep it bottled up Inside, it's just going to boil up and cause you more damage.

Take a hiatus: Wait 24 hours to calm all the way down before you take any action with another person(s).

Remember the three rings?: Do the Rings of Fire exercise mentally or on paper.

Clean up your mess: If needed, follow up with the other person(s) and address what needs to be addressed. If you need to apologize, do that, and take responsibility for what you did or didn't do. Man-up and don't let this fester any longer. And yes, sometimes you need to be the bigger person!

One thing I find helpful is to set up an agreed upon code word for you and your ex so that when things get heated, you can mention the code word and each of you will know what it means and respect it. It's basically your way of saying we need a time out so let's immediately stop everything that's going on right now. Make the code word something unusual.

How-to: Have Difficult Conversations

Many men have a difficult time talking to people about their emotions and challenges, especially when the person they need to talk to is the one triggering the issue. In the event that you need to have a difficult conversation with someone, here are some steps I suggest you follow. Being the bigger person is hard, but it is worth so much more in the long run:

Step 1: First, write down what you want to get out of the conversation to create the outcome you want. Start with the end in mind. For example, "I want to express to my ex that while she has a new boyfriend and wants to introduce him to the kids, I have some hesitation around it, and I think we need guidance around what's best for them."

Step 2: Set up a time to have this conversation in person or by phone. Provide some context explaining why you'd like to have the conversation and the outcome you want to work towards.

For example, "Hi Julie. I would like to chat with you about the kids and introducing them to your new boyfriend. I'd like to ensure that the kids are prepared for this new stage in their lives and want to make sure that both you and I have the tools to help them with the transition. Please know that I'm struggling, however I want to support you and the kids with this. Someday it will be you doing the same thing for me, so please let's work together and focus on what's best for the kids."

By doing this, you're setting the tone, context, and outcome of your conversation. You could have said, "Hi Julie, you're just about to ruin the kid's lives by introducing them to someone who I have not met and if it's anything like our friends who went through the same thing, you will cause them countless problems. I want to know who this person is and where you met him before I allow him to spend any time with my kids."

Hopefully you get the point. You're in control of how a situation is handled. You can set the tone and up the odds on the chances of success. If you find it helpful, practice the conversation with someone beforehand.

Step 3: When you have the conversation, it's always important to be calm and present, and when talking always use "I" statements versus "you" statements. For example, instead of saying "You make me feel angry and you cause me problems", try saying "I feel angry, and I'm really struggling".

By using "I" statements, the focus stays on you instead of the other person and helps to keep the conversation moving forward. Using "you" statements puts the other person on red alert and they typically feel the need to defend and protect themselves against the onslaught of accusations and blame. Yes, this is when you can activate their ego.

If all else fails, walk away. If the conversation is going sideways and derailing, just stop and remove yourself from the situation. Don't make it worse. If you've decided on a code word, use it. Get away from it all so you can regroup and address it again later. In some cases, especially high conflict cases, you may need to bring in a third party to help with effective communication. Look for a mediator or family counselor versus a family friend. And don't be afraid to ask for help when you need it. It shows you're committed to a healthy outcome and that's what matters most.

Step 4: Express gratitude. Providing that the conversation goes well and neither of you explode at the other, express your thanks and acknowledge the other person for their role in moving forward towards a more positive outcome or shared goal. This goes a long way towards building a solid foundation for you to talk to your ex in the future. This is especially important when you have kids, as there will be many future occasions in which you will benefit from speaking civilly to one another while working things out.

How-to: Handling Feedback

There will also be times when you're the one on the other end of the line and your ex wants to express their emotions or opinion about something in a passionate way. If this happens, here are some helpful ideas to keep in mind:

- Set up a time where you can do this in person or on the phone.

- Make sure you have at least 15 minutes to relax and calm down before you meet.

- When you meet, your whole goal is to listen.

Yes, I said listen and there are two modes of listening:

Listening to Learn: This gets you in the headspace of understanding what the other person is saying and why they're saying it, without you being on the defensive. The key to listening to learn is to ask questions that help you understand where the other person is coming from. If you start to defend yourself, you've slipped into "listening to respond" mode (which we'll cover shortly). Your questions need to come from a place of truly wanting to understand, not from a place of ego or inauthenticity. To deepen your listening and understanding, ask clarifying questions such as:

"Could you tell me more about 'X'?"

"Can you give me an example of 'X'?"

"What is the impact to you when 'X' happens?"

If done honestly, this shows the other person that you do care about what they're saying, and this will always help build a new solid foundation for your relationship. This is especially critical when you have kids together. Listening to learn is very powerful.

Listening to Respond: This is the opposite of listening to learn; it gets you in the headspace of defending yourself and it's the only way your ego's sense of hearing operates. Everything is perceived as an attack, and the defense lawyer in you is ready to refute anything and everything the person in front of you is trying to explain. In this state, you listen for things that aren't true and things you don't believe. You're tuned in for any points you could argue against because you have hundreds of examples of how to prove the other person wrong. For many people, this is their default listening mode and it's a big reason that so many families and individuals end up in a miserable mess of misunderstood and lost communication.

Please remember not to take things personally. When your ex is emotional and reactionary, just accept that she is behaving that way because she's going through turmoil right now. It may be projected on you but maintain perspective and know that it's her story, not yours. Don't make it about you because it's not. In order to effectively accept feedback, it's important to acknowledge that the other person has been heard. It doesn't mean you have to agree with them. But by validating and acknowledging the other person's concerns and feelings, you are showing that you're listening and that you care about what they have to say.

In Summary

Mastering your emotions gives you a form of internal control; one that will help you in creating a powerful life. Once you understand that you are the architect of your own thoughts, and those thoughts are the cause of your emotions, and those emotions are what lead to your actions, you will realize that you are in fact in the driver's seat of your life.

Understanding that you are not your emotions gives you an opportunity to create a space between being consumed by them and knowing when they pop up. Awareness of this lets you break the pattern of negative subconscious action and gives you an opportunity to learn more about yourself.

The Rings of Fire exercise gives you access to changing the internal meaning of an event, situation or thought, to one that supports living a more positive and powerful life. This process is one that can be easily done in your head or on paper, and the results are unbelievable.

When you find yourself completely overwhelmed and you feel like you can't even think, refer back to the detailed instruction list on what to do to remove yourself from the situation and take back control.

And lastly, if you need to provide feedback to your ex or find yourself on the receiving end, approach it in such a way that leads to a solid and supportive outcome no matter what the situation. You'll thank me in the future!

CHAPTER THREE:
TAKING CARE OF YOURSELF

"Make yourself a priority once in a while.
It's not selfish, it's necessary." —Karen Baquiran

Many of us neglect to take care of ourselves when life goes sideways, which leaves us lacking physical energy or the mental capacity needed to deal with what life throws at us. Failing to focus on ourselves and prioritize our own needs causes us to become depleted and overwhelmed, and thus the downward spiral begins.

Taking care of yourself, or "self-care" as it's also known, is the practice of taking proactive action to preserve or improve one's own physical, emotional, and mental health. Putting yourself first and prioritizing your mental and physical health is fundamental to rebuilding your life. It's what will give you the energy, motivation, will, and inspiration to rise up, face life, and move on.

Putting yourself first is not selfish. You actually need to take care of YOU before you can take care of anyone else. Do you remember the last time you were on a plane and they made the safety announcements? What do they tell you to do with the oxygen masks in an emergency? Run around the plane and make sure everyone else's mask is securely on before you put yours on? No. They tell you to put yours on first. Why? Because if you don't take care of yourself first, you'll be useless to both yourself and those around you. This is especially important to remember when you have kids.

In this chapter, we will get you back into shape and we will give you the tools to take care of yourself mentally, physically, and emotionally so that you're prepared to take on the world. To start with, let's talk about the fastest and most effective way to get you back to focusing on yourself – assembling a new support crew that you're going to recruit, starting today!

Building Your Own "A-Team"

When I was mentally at the lowest point of my divorce, I didn't have a clue about how to take care of myself, nor did I have the will or motivation to do it. At times though, I thought I was taking care of myself by buying a bunch of crap I thought I needed (but really didn't need), dating a lot of women, going out drinking with my buddies, and even cancelling my gym membership to save money. However, as I've grown to understand, while it may have felt good for me to do these things at the time, none of it was going to help me over the longer term.

At my turning point when I made the decision to get my life back in order, I wrote down the areas of my life that I needed help with and the names of people that I was going to seek help from. Without me fully knowing it, this formed the basis of my A-Team – a group of individuals that I was going to enlist to support me and hold me accountable while creating the life I wanted. Now it's your turn to create your own A-Team.

Before we determine the positions that you will want to start recruiting for, and to ensure that every part of your life is covered, there is one thing that we need to discuss when it comes to enlisting people for your team – 'double agents'.

Of the many things that change in the process of a breakup or divorce, is our relationships with many of our friends, family members, and co-workers. While it may feel like the world is already against you, it's important to take an inventory of your current circle of friends and extended family members and make some careful cuts of possible "double agents" from the team. When I went through my divorce, I was at first overwhelmed by the seeming outpouring of support. People I hadn't spoken to in ages came out of the woodwork to contact me and ask if I was okay and what was going on. I quickly learned the difference between concern and rubbernecking. While some of these people meant well, they simply wanted the gossip rather than to help me – they turned out to be what I call double agents. I was a spectacle, and they were craning their necks trying to get a closer look. You do not want to enlist these people on your team. Surround yourself with good, well intentioned, qualified people only! Think of your A-Team as your very own Special Forces unit; a group you carefully source to keep your life on track, equipped with paid professionals, friends and family that you know you can reach out to whenever you're struggling.

Before you recruit the best of the best, you must get clear on what positions need filling for you. In my experience, these were the roles that needed filling, however there may be others you want to create for yourself.

The Number Cruncher: Perhaps you've left a messy emotional relationship with a bank account to match. Either way, chances are that your finances will look different moving forward. It really helps to get a professional to plan and assess all things money so that you know what you're dealing with. Recruit someone that will help you put a realistic plan together for rebuilding your financial future and hold you accountable to your financial goals.

The Muscle: Consider hiring a personal trainer, signing up for classes, ordering a workout plan online, finding a local group that meets up on a regular basis, or signing up for a local event. It can be hard to find the motivation to get going, so putting a little money behind it can do a lot for your accountability and help improve your results. The gym can be a daunting place where you're not sure what to do or if you're doing it right. Find a trainer who cares about getting you healthy and let them worry about the details, so all you have to do is show up. If money is an issue, find a workout partner that also needs a kick in the backside and go for regular runs together. Trust me, you'll be doing both of you a favour!

The New Guy: You might be a little thin in the friends department after culling those double agents and losing some to your ex, so it's time to branch out and create some new friendships. As an adult, it can be tough to find and keep new friends. We get stuck with old buddies along with old habits and routines. It's difficult to change and become a better version of yourself when people only know you as the outdated one, and hold you to it. Not sure where to find new friends? Start by identifying new things you'd like to do and go from there. It's always awesome to meet new people that are into the same things as you. Sign up for classes so you can get out and meet new people. When you open yourself up to new relationships and experiences, it's amazing who comes into your life!

The Nature Buff: The healing power of the great outdoors cannot be underestimated in your recovery and the building of a better life. If you find that there aren't many opportunities or relationships you currently have motivating you to get outside, get an outdoor enthusiast on your A-Team. It helps to combine the new friend search with new activities. The more you put yourself out there and try, the more friendships will follow.

The Headshrinker: Another fantastic member to have on your A-Team is a qualified therapist or counselor to coach you through the maze of feelings and stress that will continue to surface. While friends and family can be great listeners, they might not always have the most practical solutions or training to best support you. And speaking with an impartial professional can really help. You may feel resistance to talking it out, but once you start, it will feel like a massive weight has been lifted. The more you get your thoughts out, whether on paper or out loud, the better. There are many forms of therapy so make sure you do your research.

The Colleague: When I was in the midst of my divorce and flailing at work, I asked a co-worker to help spot me because I knew I was a mess. She checked in on me and ensured I was completing all the work I needed to do. She was also there for me whenever I needed to go for a walk to get my mind off something. This may not seem like much but having someone to watch your back and keep you on track at work may help you excel or even prevent you from getting fired for doing a crappy job.

The Kid Wrangler: Children can certainly amplify this strange new world you suddenly find yourself in. All routines have gone out the window and you might default to copious amounts of TV just to keep the kids busy. We'll explore the kid zone in detail in Chapter 5, but this is a common blind spot and a great position to hire for your A-Team. This can double up as meeting a friend who hosts a kids play date or pairing up with another parent to go out on a field trip.

The Suit: If you haven't already, find a supportive, collaborative mediator or lawyer that can help you with any negotiations or legal proceedings with your ex. Please understand, finding someone who doesn't just want to fight and take your ex to the cleaners is the difference between getting through this quickly or not; and, if you have kids, having a good chance of being able to co-parent. Find someone who operates based on facts versus off your emotions. This alone will save you thousands of dollars in the long run.

The Cheerleader: Along with recruiting new friends and qualified professionals it's important to surround yourself with positive, motivating people in general who won't drain your energy and bring you down. The Cheerleader can be a role filled by multiple people and sources that provide emotional support such as a life coach or relationship expert. This should also be a role that you play in your own life by constantly seeking out things and people that inspire and support you.

The Medic: If you've not had a check-up in some time, visit a physician to make sure you're in full working order. Get a clean bill of health and rule out anything serious that might be holding you back. In addition, book an appointment to see your dentist. As members of your A-Team, your medics are there to get you, and keep you, functioning optimally.

ICE (In Case of Emergency): Always have an emergency protocol in place before you find yourself in a bad situation. Look up the local hotline number for mental health services and keep it in your wallet, add it to your contacts in your phone or post it somewhere you can easily find it. If you have a shortlist of people in your life you know you can contact in the event of an emergency, make sure their information is up to date and easily accessible. It isn't that you're planning for an accident or mental breakdown, it's that you're covering all possible outcomes like the strategic mastermind that you are. Take this seriously – it's you looking out for you. Have a plan in place.

IMPORTANT: If you feel out of control or you're going to harm yourself or anyone else, please reach out to a friend, family member, emergency hotline – anyone. If you feel like you have no one to turn to, go down to your local emergency hospital and ask for help immediately. There is absolutely no harm or shame in doing that!

Are there any other roles in your life that you think need filling? If so, make a note of those as well. Now, write down a name or names under each A-Team role. Include any persons or organizations that can help your cause. When you've finished, take a step back and admire the team you just assembled! How does it make you feel to know that you've just created a team that is going to help you get your life back on track?

The next step now is to contact each person or organization, tell them what you're up to or going through, and where you need help. Make sure you schedule regular check-ins with each of them. Commit to leaning on this team when you need help. If you've explained this concept to them correctly and why you picked them, trust me, they'll be there for you.

A-Team disclaimer: There are two sets of people who absolutely cannot be on your A-Team – your ex and your kids. Selecting these people is off limits and not OK…period!

The Daily 5

My A-Team gave me a ton of support. After spending time with each of them, it seemed like each area of my life was moving forward bit by bit. Each week, I felt like I was getting stronger mentally, physically, and emotionally. The Daily 5 is another tool that is fundamental to making sure you are taking care of YOU!

Think of the Daily 5 as a daily habit that you're going to implement to ensure that you are taking care of yourself and that you're putting the important things first. I developed this habit after getting clear on, and practicing, what I needed to focus on each and every day to get my life back on track. Considering that we all carry around the tool that we need to this everywhere we go, there is no excuse for never doing it.

The Daily 5 consists of asking yourself five questions every day. You can do this as many times as you'd like. My recommendation is that you do this at least three times each day. Once in the morning when you wake up, then again over lunch time, and then again before going to bed. However, if you ever feel out of control and your ego is trying to assimilate you, do this exercise immediately. The tool to use is actually your hand and the five questions are supported by each finger on your hand. Now hold up your hand, and as you go through these questions, hold up the corresponding finger and curl the rest down – I promise it will all make sense:

The Daily 5

Bird Flipping for Boundaries
Am I saying no (AKA fuck off) to the things/people that I need to say no to?

You're #1 - Am I putting myself first?

Put a Ring on It Am I committed to my life and my goals?

Thumbs Up Am I doing OK? Examine the reasons why or why not.

Little Changes Am I focused on the small things that over time add up to big things?

Let's take a deeper dive into each question so that you can get the full impact of doing this powerful exercise.

Thumb: Am I Doing OK?

By asking yourself "am I doing okay?" you're doing a quick check-in to ensure that you're feeling good, in that moment. If you are, that's great! If not, then you need to do something. Please don't be okay with not feeling good. You need to take some form of action and do something that will immediately change the state you're in. Here are some ideas that work really well:

- Call a member of the A-Team and ask for help.

- Remember the concept "don't ignore; explore". Get your journal out and start writing down how you're feeling, and then explore why you are feeling that way. Ask what that feeling is trying to show you or teach you. If it helps, do the Rings of Fire exercise in Chapter 2 to break the emotional meaning you assigned to it and give it another meaning that will empower you.

- Do something physical like go to the gym, do some jumping jacks, or go for a walk outside.

- Put on some of your favourite music: a song that inspires you or one that will get you singing along.

- Meditate.

- Do some relaxation breathing: sit quietly, breathe in for five seconds and then breathe out for five seconds (do this at least 15 times).

- Write down five specific things that you are grateful for in life.

Index Finger: Am I Putting Myself First? Do an honest gut check. Are you actually putting yourself and your needs first? Are you truly taking care of #1? If not, then you need to adjust your thinking and priorities, say no to some things, and ensure you are carving out time for yourself each and every day. As we said at the beginning of this chapter, taking care of ourselves, or "selfcare", is the practice of taking action to preserve or improve one's own physical, emotional, and mental health. Putting yourself first, making you the #1 priority is fundamental to rebuilding your life. It's what will give you the energy, motivation, will and inspiration to rise up, face life, and move on.

If you feel like you're not putting yourself first, then you need to ask yourself the following question: "what does putting myself first look like?" This will give you insight into what you are NOT doing. When I asked myself this question, my answer looked like this (this was copied from my journal):

- Exercise daily.

- Spend quality time with my kids where I'm 100% present.

- Always eat healthy, nutritious food with a maximum of two cheat days per week.

- Read inspirational books for 30 minutes each night before going to bed.

- Have a shower before going to bed.

- Spend quality time with friends who lift my spirits and inspire me.

- Completely stop spending time with friends who are energy sucking vampires.

- Go on a hike in the mountains once every two weeks.

- Keep my room tidy and clean – no mess!

- Go to hot yoga once per week.

- Daily meditation, gratitude exercise, and journaling .

- Review my vision board and goals once per week and schedule time to achieve them.

- Speak to my family once per week.

- Minimize looking at social media at least two hours before going to bed.

- Only speak to my ex during the day and not late in the evening.

- Have a check-up with my doctor and dentist once every six months to ensure I'm okay.

Note that this is my list; yours will likely be a lot different, and that's totally okay. I can honestly say that when I don't feel like I'm putting myself first, it is always because I'm missing out on doing a handful of these things. Once you have your list, ensure you are always carving time out for it, and you will be well on your way to making yourself a #1 priority.

Middle Finger: Am I Setting Boundaries and Saying No?

Are you allowing other people's agendas to take over your life? Are you saying yes to things that you know you should be saying no to? If you're not establishing and controlling your own boundaries, you're basically saying that other people's agendas are more important than your own, and that you're totally okay with that. It also says that you put others' wants and needs above yours. As generous as that may sound, you're doing yourself a big disservice.

Think of boundaries as a set of rules, expectations, or limits that we use to define how others should treat or behave around us. We put them in place to help us feel safe, comfortable, and secure. When our expectations are not met, we may feel threatened, upset, disrespected, hurt, unloved – the list could go on. This is why it's so important to establish boundaries.

In my experience, there are three types of boundaries – Weak, Rigid, and Healthy.

Weak boundaries are undefined, and they will always shift to accommodate bad behaviour. We typically set weak boundaries when we feel uncomfortable or threatened about a given situation or person. If you have difficulty saying no to people, this may be your default state when setting boundaries.

For example, let's say your ex is always wanting to chat with you in the evenings when the kids have gone to bed, but these conversations leave you feeling anxious as they typically end badly, which in turn keeps you awake most of the night because that's all you can think about. In this situation, your weak boundary could look something like this: "I'd rather not chat to you late in the evening as it stresses me out, however if that's the only time you can talk, then I suppose it's okay".

Weak boundaries will do absolutely nothing for you. They basically give other people permission to see how far they can push you and then walk all over you. By setting weak boundaries, you will gain no respect for your asks and wishes, all of which impacts your self-esteem and supports flaky decision making and disrespectful relationships.

Rigid boundaries are usually very well defined, immovable, and non-negotiable. These types of boundaries are typically enforced as a form of control. The problem with this is that we think by making something final, the other person will have to agree to it (as they have no other choice), however it usually ends up introducing more hostility, resentment, and anger.

Using the above example of your ex wanting to chat in the

evenings, a rigid boundary could look like this: "If you want to chat with me, you can only call me at 6:00 p.m. If you're one minute late I will not pick up the phone and if you can't do that time, too bad so sad. I'm busy so you'll need to work around my schedule". Now imagine if that boundary was forced upon you – how would you feel about it?

Rigid boundaries give no space for negotiation nor discussion and, depending on how you deliver it, could come across as being disrespectful to the other person. When that happens, they will push back and typically will turn some of their boundaries into rigid ones too!

In certain situations, you might need to be rigid, especially if the other person is taking advantage of you and offers no flexibility themselves. However, before you go there, I'd like you to consider setting a healthy boundary.

Healthy boundaries are well-defined, they support your personal values, and they are open to some level of negotiation. If a healthy boundary is communicated in a respectful way, you will usually find the other person is open to it (even if they may wish to add their two cents to it). In any case, this form of boundary should allow you to feel comfortable, confident, secure, and in turn – respected. This form of boundary goes a long way towards developing a new type of relationship with your ex, especially if you have kids to consider.

In using our example again, a healthy boundary could look like this: "Talking late in the evening is not working for me. It causes me to get anxious, and I have trouble sleeping when we get into an argument. When I have the kids, it distracts me from being present with them and that's not fair to them, nor to me. I'd like to suggest we either find a time in the day that works for the both of us, or mid-day on the weekends. Which one would work for you?".

When you imagine the responses to the examples given, you can hopefully see that there could be three very different outcomes to the same situation. So, ask yourself, which type of boundary will result in the outcome that will best support you moving on with your life? And if you have kids, which approach do you think will help start to build a strong co-parenting relationship with your ex?

Ring Finger: Am I Putting the Energy and Effort into What I'm Committed To?

When we get into a funk, we typically lose sight of, and motivation to work towards achieving the things we are committed to. This includes our goals, dreams, health, relationships, and career aspirations. When we stop focusing on these things, our lives can easily unravel, leaving us feeling like we're going nowhere.

In the next chapter we'll take a deeper dive into creating your future self and we'll help you come up with focuses and goals that support the life you want.

I once read that no matter who you are, whether you're the president of the United Stated, Spiderman, Oprah Winfrey, or the most successful person you know, we all have 24 hours in a day. Successful people choose how they spend their day – they do not let other things dictate that. When you lose focus on working towards the things that matter to you, it's not that your priorities have changed, it's just that you are not carving out the time to focus on them. Something or someone else is taking over your time and you're allowing that to happen, most of the time unconsciously. If you think back over the past seven days, how have you spent your time? What have you been doing that doesn't support the things you are committed to? For example, did you plan on going to the gym after work, but then a friend called you to go out for a drink and you chose that instead? Or maybe you had planned on taking your kids out to the zoo, but instead you decided to stay at home to watch Netflix?

There is only one person you can ever rely on to take care of you and that is YOU! Please, carve out the time to focus and work on what you are really committed to. Don't let other people and situations completely take over your life. You must stay in control and consciously choose where you spend your time and effort.

Pinky Finger: Am I Focused on the Small Things?

Are you focused on the small things you can do every day that, over time, add up to the big things? If not, you should be! And when I say small things, I am referring to actions like the following, which if you commit to doing, will bring more joy, happiness, peace, and calm into your life.

- Daily journaling: While your assumptions around journaling every day might conjure up images of your kid sister and her diary, make no mistake that getting things out of your head and writing them down freestyle, brings massive mental relief. It's a way to get the garbage out – and stay out! – of your head.

- Meditation: I'm not a meditation expert, and I first learned about it by reading the likes of Thich Nhat Hanh and Eckhart Tolle. There are endless resources out there if you'd like to dig deeper on origins and methods, but I recommend that if you're starting out, try the guided variety. Free apps (like Headspace™) offer endless options and can serve as a kind of supplemental tech on your A-Team. Try it to start and/or end your day. It's perfect for switching off that internal voice so you're not worried or stressed. Try 3-15 minutes. Doing so improves sleep, helps combat addictions, decreases blood pressure, encourages a healthy lifestyle, enhances self-awareness and self-kindness, and promotes positive emotional health. Other benefits include reduced stress and anxiety, improved concentration, clarity, happiness, and acceptance. Plus, it's absolutely free, it's portable, and can be done anywhere, anytime.

- Start your day with an intention: When you start your day by creating an intention to live by for the next 24 hours, it's important to consciously choose something that you can keep top of mind because it helps in discovering and driving each moment with purpose. It's okay to repeat the same one the next day but don't go longer than a couple of days before setting a new one. It could be something like smiling or saying thank you to three people, going for a walk, exercising, being grateful, eating healthy, helping someone in need, and so on – just a small thing that helps you focus on seeing the positive and building proof that you follow through on what you set your mind to do.

- Change your password: Credit goes to my good friend Pat who suggested this one. Make your passwords on different devices something motivational and change them each month. These can align with your intentions and be something simple. The following are examples only: f1nDL0V3, BeH@ppy, E@tG00dF00d!!, Exc3rc1seL1k3aBe@st. How many times per day do you type in your password? This regular daily reminder gets into your subliminal messaging – the good kind of brainwashing – subtly reinforcing the healthy habits you wish to create.

- Be grateful for everything: Gratitude melts away stress and worry. When writing down at least three things you are grateful for, it's necessary to get specific and really feel the emotions rather than just mindlessly jotting down a list. This can be a challenge, especially at first, or if you don't feel there's much going well in your life (let alone to be grateful for). I worked through this with a client going through a particularly messy split with an ex who had cheated. When I asked him if he could think of something to be grateful for about her it took him a lot of head shaking, resistance, and time but eventually he said, "well, she's a phenomenal mother". I was proud of him for getting there and it shifted his thinking and ability to get strong and move on. It can do this for you, too.

The Three Non-Negotiables

There are three things that make a world of difference when it comes down to your health, mood and energy levels. What you put into your mouth, how often you work out, and how much you sleep.

What you put into your mouth: If you're not feeding yourself good nutritious food, you're destroying yourself. You literally are what you eat. A poor diet will drain you of all your energy and motivation. By eating food that is full of chemicals, toxins and things you can't even pronounce, you immediately put your body into stress because it has to deal with getting rid of the shit you're putting inside your temple.

By feeding your body real food, you will provide it with everything it needs to get back into top fighting shape, giving you the energy, motivation, and good vibes for taking on whatever life throws at you. My simple recommendation is to eat "real food". Trust me, it's not complicated. If you recognize and can read the ingredients, chances are it's okay to eat. If you can't pronounce it, you probably shouldn't consume it.

How often you work out: My wife is a personal trainer, and her motto is "sweat every day". You don't need to be on a plan that turns you into Arnold Schwarzenegger; you just need to get your heart rate up for at least 30 minutes every day by doing something physical. Outside of going to the gym, try one of the following: go for a power walk, run up and down some stairs, do a filthy fifty (I'll let you Google that one!), dust off your bike and go for a ride, go for a run, play squash/tennis/badminton … you get the point. Just do something that will get your heart rate up. Just in case you need a reminder of the benefits of exercising:

- Helps reduce stress.
- Builds self-esteem.
- Improves mood.
- Helps to clear your mind.
- Boosts your immune system.
- Lowers cholesterol.
- Lowers blood pressure.
- Keeps skin and hair healthy.
- Improves sleep.
- Improves memory and concentration.
- Improves your sex life (hello!).
- Reduces inflammation.
- Need I go on?!

Everything about exercising is awesome! As it can be a social thing, maybe you'll meet someone special along the way too!

How much you sleep: The benefits of sleep are many, and as you know, after a good night's rest it just plain makes you feel better. Beyond boosting your mood and helping you look your best, the benefits of regular sleep range from improving heart health, boosting immunity, and controlling body weight, to decreasing stress and improving mood, creativity, and memory function. While there are many things you can do to help you get a great night's sleep, here are some ideas that really work:

- Shower or bath right before bed.

- Listen to some calming music as you drift off.

- Meditate to quiet the mind.

- Journal to get those thoughts out of your head and free up some space.

- No screen time at least one hour before going to bed.

- Darken your room with blinds.

- Take a brisk walk after supper.

- Wash your bed linens every few days.

Listen, stress destroys you physically and mentally. I came out of my divorce with far more grey hairs than I had going in. By eating well, exercising, and getting enough sleep, you'll be doing a lot more than the average person does in terms of taking care of #1. Remember though, feeling better takes time. I urge you to give it your best effort, and trust me, you'll feel like you're vibrating on a different level.

There are three things that you should NOT be doing as you go through this process of healing and moving on with your life, as they will inevitably stall you from moving on: don't be a loser online, don't sleep with your ex, and don't date until you're ready.

Don't be a loser online: Don't be a total jackass and vent on social media about how bad your ex might be, or how awful or awesome your life is without them. While it's still the Wild West when it comes to legal stuff around the internet, there are more and more instances of social media posts being admissible in court. In addition to this, you should never post or say anything online that could impact your kids if they were to read it, whether it's about their mom, family, friends, new boyfriend or otherwise, just keep that stuff to yourself.

Social media is a time waster and worst of all, a very inaccurate glimpse of someone's highlight reel. Paying too much attention to anyone's social media activity isn't something I recommend for your wellbeing and especially if that someone is your ex. As easy as it is to follow someone, freedom from that unhealthy obsession is just one simple click away. I implore you to delete, block, and unfollow all social media connections to your ex ending, once and for all, the creeping of relationship statuses and passive peeping of a new life that doesn't include you. Not doing so will continually fan the flames of your anger and outrage at the situation. Doing so makes you feel powerful and in control. You choose.

Don't sleep with your ex: In the case you are confused, sleeping with your ex is absolutely off the table. This includes, but is not limited to, makeup sex or any other variety of intimacy no matter how much you might miss it. You're going to be feeling a lot of emotions, and losing access to another person's life and physical connection will surface in many ways. That's fine. Let it. Understand that acting on it will derail you in more ways than you can imagine as it will end up emotionally confusing the two of you, your kids and those around you.

Don't date until you're ready: The one question practically everyone asks (especially fresh out of a breakup) is "when should I start dating again?" To which I always flip around and respond with a question of "when is it okay for people to start dating you?". While the timeline can vary, I strongly advise that if you're really serious about creating a better life, learning from past mistakes and not repeating them again, no dating for at least the first six months. It's important to focus on yourself and only date when you're truly ready. No one new wants to be your caretaker, and if they do, please run in the other direction.

When I met my wife Cara, she asked an impressive question on our very first date that has stuck with me – "what did you learn from your divorce?". Back then it floored me, but luckily, I did have some answers ready from all the painfully messy work I'd undertaken long before I said yes to that date. Asking yourself the above question and examining your answers can be a good gauge of where you're at on this journey. If all you can come up with is painting a villainized portrait of your ex and/or complete victimhood on your side, you may not pass go nor collect two hundred dollars – let alone someone else's phone number.

The Contract

Now is the time for you to truly commit to taking care of yourself and make sure you are always #1. To do this, you are going to fill out the contract below and sign it. This is your contract that you are making with yourself and no one else. No one needs to see this. This is between you, and you only. Feel free to download a copy from https://www.shesgonemoveon.com, edit it if you'd like, fill it out, print it off and then take a photo and keep it on your phone where you can see it anytime you need reminding.

Making Myself My #1 Priority

I _____ solemnly swear from this date of _____ / _____ / _____ forward, to make my needs number one. I realize the vital importance of this and vow to put myself first in a genuine way – not by distracting myself from dealing with issues or avoiding the pain. I know now, that doing so really amounts to putting myself last, and that is no longer acceptable.

It is my main focus to become a priority in my own life. To put myself at the top of my list, understanding and having faith that in doing so, the rest of my world will fall into place. My actions and intentions will align with my goal of starting to love myself because I am who I'll be spending the rest of my life with, and it's the most important relationship to continuously show up for.

I vow, going forward, to expect less from others and more from myself. I will not make myself an option, but a very top priority. Before anything else, I put myself in my own schedule. I understand there is nothing to be ashamed of when I'm struggling, and I promise to not ignore times that my body and/or mind are signaling that I need to seek help. I will willingly reach out to my A-Team when needed.

I will take care of myself and realize that if I'm not in working order – nothing in my life can work. So, I commit to tending to myself, above all and beyond anything else.

_____

(Signature)

In Summary

You need to put yourself first, period! You are responsible for you, no one else, and if you're not taking care of yourself, don't expect anyone else to do it. By putting your A-Team together, you're assembling the best of the best and surrounding yourself with people that can both help you and hold you accountable to doing the things you're committed to. They will be an invaluable team that will help you get through this, and they'll be at the finish line cheering you on as you cross over it.

The Daily 5 is a daily habit you're going to implement to ensure that you are taking care of yourself and that you are putting the important things first. All you need is your hand and the five questions to ask yourself. When you do this, it's like a daily self-check-in to ensure you're doing okay, and if you're not, you'll quickly adjust to get you back on track again.

Taking care of your health is simple. Eat healthy, sweat every day, and get your 8 hours of sleep. By doing this, you'll give yourself and your body the energy it needs to accomplish anything. It will keep you motivated and energized so that you can take on the world!

The Contract is a commitment, a promise that you are making to yourself to look after #1. This is a pledge – a vow that you are now responsible for – and after reading this chapter you now have the tools to summon the energy to see it through.

CHAPTER FOUR:
THE FUTURE YOU

"We can't predict the future, but we can invent it."
—*Dennis Gabor*

For many of you reading this book, while you go through the experience of an ended relationship, your entire identity and future plans may seem in question. You may feel like, all of a sudden, you're lost and life has no real meaning anymore. Up until now, your future may have been somewhat defined by the relationship you were once in, but now that feeling of surety and safety is in question.

Your life is now going to be different moving forward and your future is somewhat unknown. It's no longer what you assumed or maybe took for granted, and for many that can be scary. Perhaps you feel like you don't know who you are anymore, robbed of the false sense of security you once had, leaving you frozen in finding a way to move on.

When I went through my divorce, I had countless people tell me I was destined to live a life of misery. They welcomed me with open arms into the doomed fold of life after love lost. Assuring me, as experienced divorced experts themselves, that I now faced a single life full of mere survival while hemorrhaging support payments, seeing my kids 50% of the time, living in a small apartment, not having the time or money to enjoy creative pursuits or pleasures, and not being able to find a new fulfilling relationship because who would want to date a divorced guy? I was told that I would have to work the rest of my life because I wouldn't be able to afford retirement. And you know what? I believed them. Because most of the people telling me these things were in that place themselves. They hated their life, and they certainly weren't shining examples of happiness or post-loss inspiration. They gave me no hope, and for several months I took on their perspective of the world. That's when the stress of dealing with a divorce and the perceived reality of my "it's all over for me" life hit and sent me to some very dark places. Does this sound familiar?

When you look at your life now, is the future laid out before you full of excitement and challenges; driving you to live a life of purpose, determination, and no regrets? Or is it one that you don't like because it's empty; forcing you to focus on everything that's holding you back from having the things you have dreamed of, and giving you every excuse under the sun as to why things suck and are the way they are?

Mindset Over Matter

The truth is, your future hasn't happened yet, so in theory your future doesn't exist (please re-read the last sentence several times and let that sink in). Because your future hasn't happened yet, the story you've made up about what your future is going to look like, is what's determining your miserable outlook on life.

Most of your days might be spent preoccupied in a falsely perceived world that makes you scared shitless of tomorrow. You might find yourself waking up every morning asking, "what's the point of putting any effort into life anymore if the future seems so grim?". I don't blame you. Believing in a future like that does seem painful and pointless. Something needs to change. You need to change. Your mindset needs to change.

When I came across this quote from Dennis Gabor "We can't predict the future, but we can invent it", it totally rocked my world and shifted my perspective on what I was doing and what I was thinking. It gave me a feeling of comfort with the uncertainty of an unknown future and exposed me to the empowering freedom in being its creator. You can never know what life will throw at you, as you've likely experienced in the aftermath of your relationship crumbling, but you can absolutely design a future worth living for. And while you can't predict the future, you can damn well start stacking the cards in your favour.

So what future are you creating for yourself right now if nothing were to change? I'll take a wild guess that your answer is not very exciting or motivating for you. But let me ask you another question: What future *could* you create for yourself that *would* be worth living? This question opens the possibilities of what you really want in life.

Figuring out what you want in life doesn't mean looking to others, comparing their life to yours and wanting the same things they have. Have you come across that great Oscar Wilde quote "Be yourself, everyone else is already taken"? Only you can truly define what your life is all about. The good news is you now have the awareness to figure out what *does* give your life meaning and purpose.

When you have something specific to look forward to, it can serve as a lighthouse in stormy times of stress and low moods, keeping you on course and powering forward. This is something almost every truly happy and fulfilled person has in their life. It isn't that they're more motivated or have some superhuman discipline that you don't. It's that they know their purpose; they clearly know what they want and why they want those things. When we know why we're doing what we're doing to create the life we want – we're basically unstoppable. We are designed to always be reaching for something, even from day one as babies we're grasping and crying out. That hardwired seeking supercharges determination, and if you have kids and have ever witnessed them taking their first steps, you'll know what I mean. Just like an infant learning to walk, we're sure to stumble, often a lot, but when the goal is locked, loaded, and set, we will persevere until we achieve it.

As much as it might feel like it, this is not your final destination in life. So, I urge you right now – decide to stop acting like it is. And once you do, once you begin to take intentional, actionable steps towards your new future, incredible things will start to happen. Just reading this chapter doesn't mean everything will suddenly turn out the way you want it to. You must always be taking action to create that life, and when you do, you'll discover a sense of power, purpose, and motivation. When you take action, unimaginably good stuff will start to flow into all areas of your life.

The Future is Only Scary if You Avoid it

I'll call on a well-worn saying here that "things can't fester in the light". If you've been holing up in the darkness and avoiding eye contact with any semblance of a future, try simply flicking the lights on and facing it. Look at it dead on. Things that you pay attention to can't stay stuck. Avoidance ensures things carry on awful or get worse; if you're looking the other way, it's out of your hands. I urge you not to be a bystander in your own life.

If you're currently stuck with feelings of loss in a directionless, hopeless loop, it's because you're basing your wellbeing and future on your life as it is today. If you only measure your potential and what's possible in the future by what's happening in your current reality, life will never be something to aspire to improve or be motivated by. It's when you intentionally create your future that things start to shift, and you can find a way out. It may be just a faint light from the depths you're in now, but with focus and effort, including working the exercises in this chapter, you will get there. Remember that the future is only scary if you avoid it. So why not create one you can get excited about?

This is the part of the journey that makes or breaks you. It's the "turning point" in the story, the bridge that either carries you across or keeps you stuck on the side of dissatisfaction, victimhood, and sameness. If we consider this book up until now as sort of browsing or window shopping, this is the time you throw down your money and BUY – you are all in. You aren't waffling anymore, you're committed to taking action, witnessing the change that comes as a result, and building more on top of that. If up until now your version of ego John hasn't really been a bother or uttered so much as a peep – he will come charging through the gate flipping over tables and shouting in your face that you're a moron for even considering any of the recommended actions in the upcoming pages. If you're finding resistance to the activities that lay before you, it's a sure sign that there's still work to be done. And that's ok, this does not mean put the book down and give up.

Before we dive in, let's cover some non-negotiables. Choosing to not redesign your environment, mind state, and circumstances to best set you up for success before embarking on this, is like going on a road trip without first checking your tires, lights, and gas tank. You can leave things up to chance and pray for a miracle, or you can bulletproof your plan of attack to best your odds of coming out victorious.

✓ **Top-Level View**

While we're all about action in this book, it's important to first get a lay of the land and understand all the details. Read through this entire chapter before taking any action. Give your brain a chance to catch up and process the bigger why behind what you'll be doing to ensure your body will follow.

✓ **Protect Your Time**

Schedule time to complete these exercises. Right now – get your scheduling system out and block off some time over the next few weeks to bang this out. I would suggest booking several 1- or 2-hour chunks of time. You MUST protect those time blocks fiercely. The more you solidify them in whichever calendar method you choose, the more real it becomes and the more you respect the process. It's harder to go out and drink away an evening mindlessly before a blocked off morning for this. Remember, if you fail to keep your commitment, and sabotage your efforts, you won't get the results you're looking for.

✓ **Be in a Positive Headspace?**

If you're reading this and not in the best headspace, try revisiting chapter three for immediate, actionable solutions to break through that mental fog, get you thinking clearer, and feeling better.

When you should *not* do this… Immediately following a fight with your ex, on the heels of a confrontation with a co-worker, while a work deadline looms over you, on a few hours of sleep, six beers in, and so on. You get the picture. This process deserves your time and attention and you at your best.

Here are some shortcuts that may help get you there and keep you there:

Focus on this early in the morning before the day rushes in with all its noise and obligations. If you tend to be more of a night-owl and get flashes of inspiration and a second wind once the sun goes down, then do this in the quiet hours of the late night/early morning, but never sacrifice sleep.

Ensure you have space and privacy – insulate yourself from screaming kids, noisy roommates, and any external chaos. This might mean taking a field trip, ideally to somewhere awe-inspiring. For me, that was sitting by the side of a glacier lake in the Rocky Mountains. I realize not everyone has that option. You could rent a hotel room and hole up in there for a day or two, go to the garage and set up shop, or camp out in a café outside your neighborhood and enjoy the anonymity and freedom that brings. Whatever it looks like, find a separate, safe space, free of distractions in which to do this.

Some noise can be motivating if it's the right kind; inspirational music can include anything that helps you focus and doesn't distract from the main task at hand. Often ambient or classical styles without lyrics can be useful, but I've had some clients blast screaming death-metal. Do whatever works and gets you in your zone.

Remember not to rush this. Rome wasn't built in a day, and the same goes for the life you want to define and build towards. This may take days or weeks to do. As you give this process and the questions more thought, you'll begin waking up to things all around you. It's like coming out of a coma. And that can be a gradual process.

Back to Your Future

At some stage in your life, you probably had an idea of a future that excited and motivated you. One that was crystal clear in your mind of everything and anything you wanted. If someone asked you back then what you were living for, you could tell them exactly what it was and it made you proud. Unfortunately, we often forget or lose this vision of our future selves and instead we go with the flow of life. Many of the men I coach recall how their ex complained about them being boring, and the reason they decided to leave was that they wanted to enjoy life before it was too late. No matter what the reason is for your divorce, that chapter of your life may have closed, but a new one has now opened up. One that you are going to create by going back to your future.

Remember that quote, "We can't predict the future, but we can invent it"? Well, if you choose to do nothing then you'll stay stuck where you are now and you can pretty much predict your future. Remember, when nothing changes, nothing changes. Or, starting right now, you can decide to design a new future for yourself; a new life that YOU will create for you and only you. When you rewrite your future, you will naturally want and take action to move towards it, and that is where the game changes.

By the end of this chapter, you will be on your way to creating a clear, visual, detailed picture of what you want your future to look and feel like. This is a powerful exercise; one you can revisit and tweak as life unfolds to inspire you to live the life you want. It will ground you when needed, inspire you when your motivation lags, and keep you on course for a life worth living. Now, let's get to work!

Get out a pen and paper, or if you prefer, your laptop or smartphone. I advise picking up a notebook and going the old school analog method because there is something to be said for the creative science and neural pathway building of the brain/handwriting connection. However, if you choose to go digital, please shut off your device or turn airplane mode on.

Now that you're all set up, I want you to write or type this simple and powerful question:

What do I want my life to look like?

I want you to write down anything and everything that comes to mind. Don't try to make sense of it. Just write and please don't stop. Remember that ego we discussed? If you think of something and that voice inside your head tells you "there is no way you'll ever be able to do/have that", ignore it and write it down anyways. Don't hold back. When you acknowledge the mental chains that are stopping you from creating the life you want and you break free of them, it's amazing how much permission that immediately gives your mind to think freely.

Many of you might fall into the trap of making this simple question more complicated than it needs to be. Attributing more difficulty to it because you think "it can't be that easy" is one of ol' ego John's most impressive forms of deflection and creative procrastination. Overthinking this makes it nearly impossible to finish and can mean giving up and not forging onward. So, let's just stick to the simplicity of this and not heap on anything extra. Consider the question again:

What do I want my life to look like?

Ready, steady, write! Whatever just popped into your mind, write it down. I don't care how stupid, silly, or unreasonable it may be to you, just write it down and it will give space to the next thought.

If you're still struggling to find answers, try taking a trip to your local bookstore and look through the magazine section. Take in all the images and topics covering fitness, money, photography, politics, gardening, wildlife, parenting and so on. Write down everything you see that makes you say to yourself "I'd love that in my life". If you can, buy a couple of the magazines that really stand out to you. There are digital alternatives to this too, but be cautious – we're inundated with images online, and it can end up sucking you down a toxic comparative vortex.

If your mental creative juices are still not flowing, try asking yourself these questions:

- If nothing could stop me from having the life I want, what would my life look like?

- If a magic genie granted me 10 wishes, what would I want them to be?

- If I were to read/write my eulogy, what would I want it to say about my life?

- What did I used to think and dream about back in the days?

Remember, just keep writing – don't stop. Just keep going and write anything and everything that comes to into your mind. When nothing else is coming to your mind, it's time to switch gears. Remember, you can come back to your list another time and continue to fill it out.

Let's take this one step further

Now that you've got an idea about what you want your overall life to look like (and well done, by the way), let's take this one step further and dive deeper into some key areas of life:

- Health & Fitness
- Mind & Emotions
- Family & Friends
- Money & Finances
- Fun & Experiences
- Career & Business
- Growth & Development
- Relationships & Love

For each key area of life, I would like you to go deep and ask yourself the same question – "What do I want my life to look like?" If you're not sure where to start, start with the area that you think needs the most work. For example, if your Family & Friends are in a good place but your Money & Finances isn't looking great, then start with that one! If you're looking at this and feeling a little overwhelmed, plan to tackle one area a day for the next eight days. Keep that notebook close to you at all times as you never know when inspiration may hit you.

"Life isn't about finding yourself. Life is about creating yourself." —George Bernard Shaw

As you're going through the exercises in this chapter, have you noticed a moment or two where you are free of worrying about all the shit going on in your life? If you look inside, you might feel a new positive sensation of motivation and focus. Doing the work in this section can mean the difference between waking up each morning feeling stuck, fixated on your ex, financially stressed and out of options – to feeling ready to tackle the core issues and move through each minute of each day with focus, purpose, and excitement.

There are no quick fixes here. It's natural when we're in pain and discomfort to seek readily available solutions to numb it out. That's why so many cases of addiction occur, and why more second marriages fail than first ones – we often jump into anything just to escape a current hell. What we don't take time to notice is that we're falling further down into a worse reality, making it that much harder to climb out. Seeking out temporary distractions and Band-Aids only compounds the hole you're in. Waking up stuck in the past can make it hard to move, let alone strive for more. But when you start doing the work outlined in this book, you create space. Space in your crowded mind and your physical existence for a better reality to move towards and thrive.

Your New Reality

So far, you've built up a library of notes around what you'd like your life to look like. Now it's time to take those notes and turn them into a narrative for your "future story". Now before ol' ego John starts drowning us out here, you absolutely do not have to be any kind of a creative type to accomplish this. It's simply an exercise in storytelling. And rest assured, deep down you are a proficient storyteller. We tell ourselves and others stories all day, every day. Part of the reason you're here, striving for better is because you're sick of the elaborate future-life-stopping stories you've become such an expert at repeatedly telling yourself! Now it's time to write a new one.

When you write down the stuff you want, it subconsciously tells your mind what to focus on so you can filter out all the other noise. Trust me, just reading this is a great start, but as life goes on, it can be easy to forget and often it slowly fades into the background. Just like reading any motivational book, you feel great after reading the first few chapters (because you picked it up when you needed it) but then life gets in the way as it always does, and the book gets demoted to a paperweight collecting dust. Let's not let that happen this time. This time can and will be different for you.

Now that you have a good idea of what kind of future you want in each of those key areas, it's time to bring your future to life. Doing the previous exercise was the perfect start; Now your new life needs to be consistently front and center, all the time. Creating easy cues to launch you into and maintain your optimal state is key in making this work. What we'll focus on next is creating ideas for fast access anytime to safeguard you from slipping into old habits and toxic thinking patterns and help raise your frequency. Here are the three powerful assets we'll work at creating to help you do just that:

Your Future Map (AKA, a vision board) serves as a visual roadmap and reminder for your future – it outlines everything you want to obtain and achieve in one place, available at an easy glance. Like an Army General, every great strategist has a map laid out before them. You need to build that map and fill it with visual cues to keep you focused and on the path to winning what you want.

Your Future Map brings to life all the things you've thought of and written down so far about your future. It's a visualization of all those pieces you've discovered that are so important to moving forward. It serves as a snapshot, a visual cue and top-level view of where you are headed. It's your map, your final destination, keeping your thoughts and emotions aligned with, and open to all the positive things coming your way. Design your Future Map using whatever medium you choose. Here are two examples:

Analog: You can use a cork board or paper as a background to attach items you print or cut out. Use anything that jumped out at you on your recon mission from the magazines you brought home or online. Make it a mixed medium of whatever you find that speaks to you. Sketch things by hand if you like and get creative. Keep in mind that no one else ever needs to see this.

Digital: For a digital representation, find what you want online, and use the copy/cut/paste functions. Tools like PowerPoint allow you to drag images and text right into your document. It doesn't have to make sense to anyone but you; just grab the images and text you want.

Suggested items to include in your Future Map:

- Pictures of people, things, places
- Experiences (e.g., someone in a boat, or winning a race crossing the finish line)
- Symbols that evoke a feeling for you (e.g., a tiger symbolizing strength)

- Affirmations

- Inspirational words

- Quotes

Aim to keep it neat and to the point; one item (like a picture) to represent each idea or key area of your future. It's an iterative process and the sky's the limit; get as creative or minimalist as you like. You'll find things jump out at you as you read the newspaper or stare at a certain sentence on a junk mail flyer – there's no shortage of inspiration once you start looking.

Specificity is key. Displaying your aspirations visually brings them to life; it gets you one step closer to achieving them, and it informs the direction in which you want to go. The Universe will start providing you with ways to get there a lot quicker because you've clearly stated your desires and intentions.

Again, it's up to you if you want to share what you've created. It's meant as a visual asset for your eyes only so feel free to keep it that way. But displaying your Future Map somewhere prominent certainly helps keep it top of mind. Maybe that means it's posted up in your private den or office, or maybe it's in the back of your closet so every morning when you push your clothes aside you see it there; your secret with the Universe. Take a picture of your Future Map and use it as a desktop image on your computer and wallpaper on your phone. Keep copies at work, in your car, in your work and workout bags. That way you'll always have it with you and can keep referring to it. Like smelling salts to a prizefighter, you're cutting through the noise and clutter and creating something to keep you focused. An asset that at a quick glance will bring you back on track.

You may wish to try taking the pictures in your Future Map and adding them to a movie with music. iMovie has easy drag and drop features for this and endless options to add music and effects. You can even use PowerPoint. Add your favorite songs as the soundtrack to pump you up. Then once you've got your final cut, watch it. And watch it again. Try starting every morning with it. Before you do anything else, give yourself something to focus on and aspire to. It will greatly impact the direction of the rest of your day.

You can't control everything that happens, but you can control how you react – and starting from a place where you're primed and in your most positive, forward-focused mindset, benefits everyone around you. Aside from kick starting your day, your highlight reel can be the shift you need when you're feeling down, negative, or emotional. Defining what your focus is, and then concentrating and working relentlessly on it is what great Olympic athletes and successful individuals in every field do.

Sticky Note to Self. Short of becoming the guy in the movie "Memento" who tattoos daily reminders all over his body, make sure the well of inspiration that helps you stay the course doesn't run dry. Pick up a bundle of sticky notes and on each one, write down a powerful reminder of the future you want and place those suckers everywhere. Stick one to your bathroom medicine cabinet, on mirrors, inside the fridge, on the dashboard of your car, hide them in your pockets – places your sight generally gravitates to, or that you'll forget about and find unexpectedly. Ensure a steady stream of motivational reminders are literally staring you in the face and turning up when you need them most.

Quarterly Review. Schedule in your calendar three months from now to review your Future Map. Just like when you first did this, it's important to conduct your review in a proper mind state (i.e., don't do it on a weekend when you have your kids unless you want to include them in this exercise. Careful though, they might want to do one for themselves. It's contagious!) Scheduling in and circling back to reassess your Future Story and Future Map every quarter ensures you're moving in the right direction and enables you to change things up as your life changes. For example, you may have put down that you want a new career, one that excites you and makes you a ton of money. As part of you kicking ass and taking action, you've narrowed it down to a specific industry that you want to focus on. It's a steady process that you revisit and refine over time, and one you can measure the results of and build evidence upon to keep you rising to the very top.

In Summary

Understanding that your future hasn't happened yet is powerful to remember as we often get caught up in the notion that what our life looks like today is going to predict and define our future. While there is truth to that notion if you decided not to change anything, you now know that you have the power to design your future. Remember the quote from Dennis Gabor "We can't predict the future, but we can invent it".

If you choose to invent a great future, you need to explore a key question – "What do I want my life to look like?" – in all the key areas of your life. This gives you an opportunity to provide some specificity in each of these areas, which gives your future a lot more focus and meaning. The quote from George Bernard Shaw explains this perfectly – "Life isn't about finding yourself. Life is about creating yourself".

Once you are clear on what you want in each aspect of your life, you need to ensure you are taking action to create that future and maintain the focus and energy towards that life daily. To do this, creating a visual map that you can carry around with you everywhere helps you stay on target, giving you absolutely no excuses to fall off the journey of your new life.

A common theme amongst successful and happy people is their

commitment to act. Reading this book is only one step that gets you moving towards the life you want. The other steps are taking massive action towards that life. This is where the proverbial rubber meets the road.

CHAPTER FIVE:
DON'T DIVORCE YOUR KIDS

"Divorce is a journey that the children involved do not ask to take. They are forced along for the ride where the results are dictated by the road their parents decide to travel." —Dianne Greene

If you have kids, a divorce or breakup will result in changes to your family unit. It's important to remember that while things are ending with your ex, you're not ending your relationship with your kids. Moving forward, things will be different for everyone involved and yes, it will require you to evolve and adapt to how you and your ex parent, but please, I beg you, don't divorce your kids. The natural instinct for many men is to retreat in pain and lick their wounds without giving any consideration to the impact on their kids. I plead with you to fight against that urge, not just for yourself but for your kids. There will be times when you'll feel like you're barely managing, but now more than ever you need to walk that tightrope, finding new, healthier, better ways of caring for yourself, and your kids.

Even though you may be struggling, your kids are also being dragged into this unfamiliar post-breakup world. Whether they're babies, teens, or even completely grown up, seeing Mom and Dad separate will be hard on them. While statistically, separation and divorce are becoming the norm nowadays, unfortunately there are more bad stories than good ones as to how things end for everyone involved. Always stay conscious of the fact that you are not the only one going through the loss of a relationship. Your kids are going through challenges too and we can easily forget this as we deal with and process our own crap. At a time when kids, especially young ones, are forming beliefs and views about the world, having life as they know it come to a halt so drastically can have long-lasting effects. While you may not feel like it, it's crucial you step up as a parent now more than ever.

Parents separating can sometimes result in children losing regular contact with either their mom or dad, and sadly it's often the dads that drop off in that equation. Researchers have found that many children feel a loss of closeness with their fathers after their parents separate. In this time of upheaval, parental separation is just one of the many stressful events going on for children. Accompanying stressors like changing schools, moving to a new house, living with one frazzled parent, witnessing new financial hardships, and more can pile on. The first couple years following parental separation are said to be the most stressful and considering the rate for second marriages occurring within four to five years after divorce, there are also challenges of an ever-changing family dynamic. Suddenly kids may be inheriting a new step-parent as well as step-siblings.

Here's what I wish I could tell all the fathers going through divorce (well, more like shake by the shoulders and shout in every stunned face): PLEASE DON'T TOSS YOUR KIDS TO THE SIDE WHILE YOU GO THROUGH YOUR OWN CRAP! BE A MAN! BE A FATHER! LOVE THEM WITH EVERYTHING YOU'VE GOT!

No matter what the circumstances or reasons, when parents split up, a child's world falls apart. Mentally supporting and protecting your child is tough and we often forget the importance of it in the upheaval of everything else. We think our kids are either too young to understand what's going on so they won't be affected, or old enough that they can handle it. The truth is, we need to support and guide our kids through this regardless of their age, and as their parents, it's our responsibility and obligation to help them. They look to us for guidance and comfort and if we're not there for them, they start making up their own narratives to explain what's happening, leaving them to feel alone, responsible or even unloved. Don't leave your kids on their own to make sense of what's happening around them. Support, guide, and love them.

Just because you're hurting doesn't mean you can ignore your kids or pass them off to another parent or family member, expecting them to do all the work to ensure your kids are OK and healthy. Sure, there might be times when you need your space, but you are the father, so make sure you behave like one. There is nothing manly about disowning your kids or expecting the other parent to raise them until you can come back when you feel like it. This can be one of the most heartbreaking times in a child's life, especially when they are young. Kids may not show it at the start, but it can, and likely will, cause problems in their future.

However, please understand that going through a separation or divorce doesn't mean that your kids will be screwed up for life. The point is to recognize the risks and do your best to safeguard you and your family from them. None of this is easy. It takes a strong man to focus on his kids and keep going when he's down; to kick all the baggage aside and pay loving attention to the little and big ones in front of him. Parents who pull this off and do a good job of managing the moving pieces and stresses of a divorce for their children, are often surprised by how quickly and positively kids adapt.

Focusing on your kids is especially hard when you're having to deal with your own crap, and trust me when I say it's tough to step out of your own story to help your kids out. We can't project our own troubles, stories, fears, and worries on our children; they are not our sounding boards, psychologists, or support team. They need you, their dad, to be strong and provide them with comfort, hope, and most importantly to stay connected and be present with unlimited love. They need to be everything you're focused on. They need to be your world.

I'm not a child psychologist or doctor, but I have been to there with my kids and I'm still deep in the trenches here with you, navigating the maze of raising my own kids post-divorce, including now having a blended family. I know the nightmarish shock of going from being full-time in my kids' lives to adjusting to shared custody and struggling to balance my own needs with theirs. However, I am here to tell you what it's like to be a dedicated father, invested in the physical, mental, emotional, and spiritual health of my children and myself. The two paths are not mutually exclusive, on the contrary, they're inextricably linked.

Changes in Your Children

Noticing changes in your child's behaviour is very normal during a divorce. Depending on the age of your kids, they'll go through their own journey of "whys" and "what ifs", and experience fear of what the future looks like from their perceptive. It can be scary for them, and they will look to you and the other parent for support, guidance, reassurance, love, and connection. If the support isn't there, they'll find other ways of dealing with it themselves; depending on age, this could show up as shutting off all communication, running away, drugs, drinking, hanging out with the wrong types of friends, eating disorders, smoking, and a host of other unhealthy activities.

Raising kids is hard enough on a good day, but on the heels of a family separation, the importance is greater than ever to be there and pay attention to their behaviour. Depending on the age of your kids, they'll react differently with dependence intensifying in younger children and a desire for independence increasing in adolescence. For a young child, you are their entire world. For adolescence, they're starting to build a world of their own full of friends and a social life that extends beyond home. Undesirable behavior is usually a cry for help, and you need to be acutely aware when this is happening.

For younger kids, a divorce can shatter trust around dependency. No longer are the two main adults in their life behaving the way they've always known them to behave. They lose stability and don't know who to depend on. Things feel different and the outside world confirms it with new routines such as being shuttled to and from two separate households. All these changes can foster insecurities and disappointments such as when seeing one parent means not being able to spend time with the other. For younger children, when a family splits up, their longing to feel connected kicks into overdrive, and regression to an earlier form of dependency can flare up. Your child might be clinging to you desperately, panicking and vying for attention through various unhealthy forms of behaviour.

If you have older adolescent kids, rebellious behaviour and aggression tend to come out in full force. You might notice a complete disregard for the rules and traditional ways of doing things now that other systems have broken down. They may become hypersensitive to broken promises, collecting evidence that you can't be counted on for anything. They might even start to lash out at everything and everyone around them. An older child may see the breakdown as a signal that you or your ex can't be trusted to take care of the family, and they might start relying more on themselves and behaving selfishly. It can be an eye for an eye mentality, demonstrating their hurt and one-upping the damage.

It's very normal for kids to struggle immediately following a parental separation, but if their behaviour or moods persist, don't hesitate to seek professional help. Do some research to find someone in your area that can help, talk to other parents for referrals and ask around until you find a therapist that you connect with. Ideally, you want the other parent on board with this, so having a talk with them first and then going to see a specialist together can help you both help your kids. Impartial, qualified professional therapists can bring different perspectives to situations, and this can help you and your kids move forward in a positive way.

The Three R's (Routines, Rituals, Reassurance)

As your children are faced with new challenges, it's important to establish as much stability and routine as you can, as quickly as possible. Following the popular formula known as the "Three R's" will help you restore your child's trust in dependence, security, and familiarity.

Routines: As regular routines may have to be reconfigured, it's important to establish new and secure ones as soon as possible at both new households. While you likely won't agree with your ex on everything when it comes to co-parenting your child, as much as possible try to create, schedule, and stick to routines to help kids have some stability in a time of such uncertainty.

Rituals: Along with solidifying routines, create new family rituals or traditions to help replace some old ones. This doesn't have to be elaborate. It could be as simple as establishing a new dinner routine where you get the kids involved in choosing one or two dinners a week, and have them help prepare it; or maybe you go for a 30 minute family walk before bedtime, and talk about two things you're grateful for. Create routines that they'll cherish and remember for many years.

Reassurance: Don't underestimate the value in simply stating plainly and often to your kids that it's going to be OK. They look to you for guidance and information on how to feel about situations, so while it's important not to give anyone false hope around a reconciliation, remember to regularly assure your kids that despite things looking different now, they will be all right and are very loved.

When parents split up, it can be an especially sad, stressful, and confusing time. At any age, kids may feel shocked, uncertain, or angry at the prospect of their mom and dad separating. While it's normal for a child to grieve the breakup of the family, as a father, there's plenty you can do to make the process less painful for them. This can be a big challenge especially with high conflict divorces/breakups as emotions can take over your logical thinking, however emotional mastery is the key in all of this.

Co-Parenting

Before we dive into co-parenting, I want to point something out. A spotlight is now shining on you and your ex showcasing how to deal with conflict and with everything on your plate. You need to always keep in mind that your kids will learn from how you and your ex behave. As your kids grow and find their way in the world, they will have conflict in their lives too, and how they deal with it will have come from watching you and your ex deal with your divorce and relationship. Think about the bigger picture and please realize the impact you are going to have on your children – for better or worse. It's a big deal to understand this. You're laying the groundwork today for how your kids will deal with their own conflicts tomorrow. So, what are you teaching them? Are they learning to shout and argue, to ignore, trash talk someone, hang up in a huff, and shut down, or are they learning sympathy, patience and understanding?

Work With Your Ex. It's not easy to stick to things like the Three R's when one parent isn't on board. Do as much as you can to work together and never argue in front of the kids. If you see behavioural changes in your kids, let the other parent know. If you and the other parent can work together to help raise the kids, it can make a world of difference in terms of them adjusting to all the new realities. So much will change for them and if you both can make the transition smoother and less impactful, you'll all be better off.

This doesn't mean telling your ex how to parent, but it helps to agree on a basic system so kids don't have rules at one house and not at the other. Stability and consistency are so important when kids are going back and forth. Having different toys, clothes, rules, diets, punishments, and expectations when they are with mom vs when they are with dad can all be very overwhelming. The more consistency you can provide in these areas, the easier the transitions will be for your kids. Christmases and birthdays will also be different, however when they figure out that they get two sets of gifts and birthday cakes, they'll adjust.

Consistency is Key. Rules, expectations, and consequences need to be the same as much as possible. Punishments such as taking away electronics for a couple days, should be observed at the other house as well. Co-parent as best you can with open communication about what's going on with the kids to help support the other parent. When my kids were younger, my ex and I used to get together regularly to talk about the kids, what we were noticing in them, and what they were up to. As challenging as this can be, you must keep your kids mental and physical wellbeing front and center.

You could even keep a journal that the kids fill out, sharing what you did together to show the other parent and help bridge gaps and catch up on the precious time you're both missing. It also shows that you're communicating with each other and that you both care. Just be careful that you don't use it to one-up the other parent, for example: mommy took the kids to a petting zoo, now you want to take them to Disneyland. Don't do things that pressure the other parent to compete like taking the kids to places you have access to that the other parent doesn't. If the kids are going back to the other parent and asking why they can't take them to private tennis lessons, think about how that could affect the other parent. I'm not suggesting that you have to run everything by one other, just be mindful. In my case, when we put the kids into camps, both myself and my ex told the kids that both mommy and daddy are doing this for them.

Help the other parent where you can – it's just a good karmic thing to do. For example, if the other parent wants to go out on a night that she usually has the kids, maybe you can swap a day with her. Things like this go a long way in building good karma between you and your ex (of course first making sure the kids are comfortable with the switch). Try and establish some ground rules on parenting, and if it's impossible, you may have to get help with this. Explore family therapists and impartial third parties to help reach an understanding you both can feel good about.

The Right Questions. Check in with your kids on a regular basis to see if they have questions about all the changes that are happening with your family. It can help to set up a code word if they're old enough, that they can use to signal to you when they need or want to talk. Be careful about the questions you ask when you see your kids. Never ask a question that leads to something negative being said about the other parent or their friends and families. For example, don't ask "do you know why mom left me?". This confuses kids beyond your imagination, and it can, and will, cause all sorts of issues as they try to come to terms with their parents no longer being together.

Some Things Are Best Left Unsaid. Your kids may or may not ask a lot of questions about your separation, and when they do you don't need to share the whole story with them. They need to know enough so that they feel as though their questions have been answered, but they don't need to know every detail. If you're on good terms with your ex, try agreeing on how to frame the story of your breakup for the kids. Don't lie to them, always be truthful within reason, and frame things in a context that is supportive. For example, let's say your spouse had an affair. Don't tell the kids "your mom slept with some idiot". Instead, explain that you both had your differences and decided it would be best if you separated and lived your own independent lives. And never give your kids false hope that you and your ex will fix the relationship. Be honest and age appropriate.

You Can't Parent the Other Parent. Remember though, you can only control you and your actions. Trying to control the other parent will be impossible so don't set yourself up for failure by expecting that. As frustrating as it can feel at times, the other parent can, and will, do things differently, and a big part of moving forward and doing the best job you can is letting that go. Obviously, when it comes to putting your child in legitimate danger, that's a different story and you absolutely should step in. Know that things will change as time goes on and you'll need to adjust many times to the new realities that life will throw at you, like new relationships (for you or your ex), moving houses, career changes, dating, money/finances, blended families, extended families, and so on.

Experiences Over Stuff

Your kids get only one chance to be kids, so let them have their time and opportunity to experience life as a child. What you do or don't do now will have a far-reaching effect on the lives of your children – both good and bad. A lack of money or time isn't an excuse; there are plenty of free things to do and if you can't get to activities during the work week, you always have weekends, so show them a great time that they will remember – and that doesn't mean big or expensive things. There are plenty of arts and crafts, gardening and new household renovation projects, baking, and endless other inexpensive but memorable activities to try. One father I met, who was at a loss for what to do with his young child, stopped off at a local craft store and picked up some inexpensive supplies. He spent time with his daughter crafting a card she could give to her mom. His little girl was so proud and excited to give it to her. Imagine the impact that had on both the child and the other parent.

Other ideas could be doing something as simple as going down to the river to feed the ducks and throw stones in the water, going to a friend's house for a play date, or having the kids help you cook a dinner of their choosing. If you find that they're not interested in doing a specific activity, then offer them a few choices. If that doesn't work, sometimes you'll need to respectfully cut off all the electronics, coax them out of their bedrooms, and get them doing something that you've picked. They may appear to not appreciate that in the beginning, however they'll start seeing the fun in it soon enough. The future outcome of what you do and how you handle things as a father now, may not be easy to see immediately. It may take your kids years to understand the effort, or ever say thank you for loving them through one of the most traumatic times in their lives. They may never say thank you, however when they're all grown up and have healthy friends, families, and relationships, just know that a part of that will be because of you, their father, putting in the hard work you are now.

Quality One-to-Ones. If you have more than one child, please ensure you schedule quality one-on-one time with each child separately. This was an idea my ex gave me, and it was brilliant. Carving out special time for you and your child to spend together away from their siblings is such a powerful way of demonstrating to them how much they mean to you. Even though I got divorced many years ago, my kids still talk about the times we spent separately together. And please when you arrange this time, make it an experience your kids look forward to and not dread.

Creating Positive Memories for Your Kids. Everything you say and do will impact your kids, so always do your best to avoid creating disappointing events, like not showing up when you said you would. It's important to plan stuff to do with your kids. Having a night in is OK here and there, but if you're not doing anything with them, they will get bored. It's so easy to quickly slip into a sad routine of picking them up exhausted from school and plopping them in front of the TV while you continue working. Suddenly it's time for bed and that's it. Sure, this scenario will happen now and then with any busy life, but if it becomes the norm, your kids will wind up preferring their time spent at the other house. Be fully present when you have them. Don't put the TV on to distract them or give them unlimited electronic time. Kids learn how to deal with this whole situation by what you're showing them, so don't teach them to be a zombie and get lost in the world of social media, TV, and computer games.

Every bit of time you get with your kids should be spent creating worthwhile experiences. Consider baking cookies at home, gardening, painting their bedroom together, planting a tree in the backyard – caring for it and watching it grow over time. A great, fun, loving childhood is something we all want to experience and remember. Dragging your kids through your negative experience of separation is not fair and certainly not something that will build great memories.

Keep Your Questions to Yourself. Bombarding your kids with questions about what the other parent is up to is not cool. Interrogating them about what mom is up to and who's been round her house, or what time she goes out and comes back, is just childish. Never subject your kids to that type of environment or line of questioning. If you have a question that you want answered, ask your ex!

Healthy Kids = Happy Kids. Keep your children's minds, bodies, and spirits healthy by feeding them good food, getting them outdoors, taking them on adventures to get their hearts pumping, and having meaningful conversations. Maybe in your old life you didn't do much of the grocery shopping or cooking but defaulting now to ordering out every night or stocking your house with junk food will have a negative effect on everyone. There are several ways to make eating healthy food fun. Take the kids shopping with you and have them help pick out good, nutritious foods. Try giving them the task of finding a recipe online before you go out and make some of their meal ideas too. And please ensure that everyone is getting some exercise. We all know the benefits of regular exercise; and these benefits are even greater for kids. If your kids are young, try simply going for a walk, jumping on a trampoline, running around and playing at the local park, or play fighting with daddy. Or if they're old enough, try taking them down to the gym with you to work out together. Your kids can be a huge source of inspiration and you have an opportunity to be a great role model for them when it comes to health.

Kids Edition A-Team. As you work to build your own A-Team of qualified experts and support systems, why not build one for your kids as well? Start with family members who love and support you. They can help take care of the kids when needed, distract them with activities, and check in to see how they're doing. From there, other A-Teamers such as parents of your child's close friends, teachers, and coaches can be added. Building a team of support for your child can really help in times of need, like when you don't feel like you're firing on all cylinders or when your child doesn't feel comfortable talking directly to you about certain things.

I know you'd like to think that you can solve everything being a guy and all, however because you are so close to your kids, sometimes you might be the last person they want to talk to. Kids don't want to upset their parents, so they may avoid speaking up about issues, especially after the turmoil of a family split. When you ask your kids how they are doing, you might get the "I'm fine" response, when deep inside they are hurting or struggling. Having a trusted third party they can talk to is a great way for kids to open up and help you support them.

Have friends who also have kids get involved too. I know when I expanded my group of friends, some had kids that I was able to arrange play dates with. It allowed my kids to take their minds off the divorce and just be kids. If possible, have your children hang out with other children from separated families (providing they are good examples) so they can have a positive reference to the whole mom and dad separating situation. It's a great context to give them glowing examples of different family situations.

Whether or not teachers or coaches from your child's school make it onto their A-Team, it's important to let the school know about what's going on so that they can be on the lookout for changes in your child's behaviour. It's amazing what teachers can pick up on. They can keep an eye on schoolwork, attitudes, and friendships – all of which can be signs of how your child is struggling or thriving.

Part of your A-Team doesn't even have to be another person – it can also be an age-appropriate book that focuses on dealing with emotions, divorce, or living in different houses. These types of books help kids feel like they're not so alone and can provide answers to challenges they might be going through.

The Two Most Common Questions

Here are two questions I get asked a lot from men when it comes to handling children:

Q: How do I introduce my kids to my new partner?

A: Introducing your kids to a potential step-parent is no small feat and it shouldn't be taken lightly. My cardinal rules, before you introduce them to a partner, are as follows:

- You must have dated this person for at least six months. Don't introduce them to someone that you've only known for a week even though you think you might be in love.

- Before you introduce your kids, always let the other parent know that you intend on doing this. This isn't about getting permission; it's about maintaining open lines of communication, and ensuring a "no surprises" experience for your ex.

- Spend time considering how your kids might react. This will allow you to let them know in a way that hopefully resonates.

- When you tell the kids, do it by yourself (without your new partner present). Have an age-appropriate conversation with them, and if you have multiple kids you may decide to have separate conversations.

- Let your kids know that you have been seeing this person for some time, that you would like to introduce them, and why.

- Ask if this would be OK and if they have any questions about this person. If they're not comfortable about meeting your partner, leave it and come back to it later. Don't push the conversation or make them feel bad for saying no. If they are comfortable, ask them when and where they would like to meet this person.

- Always acknowledge and thank them – even if the conversation doesn't go well.

Make sure your new partner knows enough about your kids so

that they can reference things when they finally meet, for example: "Sophie, your dad has been telling me so much about your dancing competitions". When your partner meets your kids, make it somewhere fun and casual like a market or a park; if the kids feel uncomfortable, they can focus on something fun around them instead of going to hide in their rooms. Your kids won't likely love your new partner on day one. Take it easy and slow – these things take time.

Q: What do I do if my ex is saying bad things about me to the kids?

A: This is a very common issue and is a trigger for so many guys. First off, don't react to it; don't take your anger or frustration out on your kids who are confiding in you.

- Empathize with your child about how hard it is to hear something like that from the other parent.

- If possible (and truthfully), correct any misinformation while ensuring it's age appropriate; be mindful that you're not doing what the other parent just did to you.

- Thank your child for letting you know and remind them how important it is to share their concerns.

- Never minimize the impact that this behaviour has on your child.

- Remember this is a conversation for you and the other parent; never make it your kid's fault, or they won't want to share anything with you again.

In general, there are two ways most people tend to react to hearing that their ex has been saying bad things about them to their kids:

Passive, where they minimize the significance of what was said or happened. If you don't like conflict, this may be your go-to response.

Pissed off, where they launch into beast mode and purposely take the other parent down too. If you're angry, hurt, and generally defensive, this may be your go-to response.

However, there is a third, more powerful, way to deal with this that I'd like you to consider:

Chill and supportive, where you provide a controlled, loving, non-defensive response that does not throw the other parent under the bus.

An example: "Daddy, mom says that when you left us you took all the money and that's the reason she can't put us into summer camps this year or even take us on a vacation."

Your passive response could be: "That's silly darling. I'll make sure you have a great summer."

Your pissed off response could have been: "Your mom is lying, and she is full of it. You should ask her about the money she stole from us which I know she's selfishly spending on herself. Or ask her where all the money I pay for child and spousal support goes. I give her more than 50% of what I make so I wouldn't trust anything she says."

Your chill and supportive response may have sounded like this: "I'm sorry that mommy is sharing that with you. These are adult issues, and she should be discussing her concerns with me and not you. It's true that since our divorce, both of us have less money to live on and we are both doing the best we can to ensure that you have everything you need. Everything will be OK and we love you."

Can you see the difference?

It's important that you don't ignore behaviour like this. Arrange a time to talk to your ex and be open about how this is affecting the kids (remember, make it about them and not you). Please don't launch into a battle and argument; if she gets defensive, keep your calm and try not to engage. Raise your point in a constructive and supportive way – that's your goal. Make it known that you are not OK with what she said, and let her know what you communicated to your child. If the other parent is having a hard time understanding this, try to flip it and ask how saying bad, confusing, nasty things about her to the kids would make her feel. If she's unconvinced, suggest getting some help so that you can deal with this as co-parents. If need be, you may need to send your child to get help so that they have the tools to deal with this.

Whether you are with your kids or away from them, you are always their father. Text them to say you love them; pick up something small but meaningful to give them when you see them next to let them know that you're always thinking about them. While you may not be under the same roof as your kids all the time now, you're always their dad, so make sure they know that. If you're away from them for long periods of time, stay in touch. Technology allows you to stay connected from anywhere, so there are no excuses; just be respectful of the other parent's time with them too.

You're not in a competition with the other parent. All you can do is your best and if your best isn't getting the results you want, don't be afraid to get help. There is absolutely no shame in bringing in professionals, especially when it comes to ensuring your kids are alright. Remember, this is about them and not you. You are not failing as a father if your kids are struggling – it's expected that they will have trouble accepting their mom and dad separating. However, ignoring that they are struggling and not doing anything about it is just not OK. No one is perfect. People make mistakes. If you screw up with something (e.g., say the wrong thing, upset one of your kids, you're late picking them up, etc.), own it, take responsibility, and address it. Remember the Manning Up chapter? If not, go back and read the damn thing! Be a powerful father, love them a ton, and let them be kids.

In Summary

For some, it's a natural instinct, when going through emotional distress, to retreat from your children in an attempt to protect them from seeing you go through what you're experiencing. It's something I've seen countless men do while going through divorce, and it's a massive mistake. Please don't wait until you feel better and have some abstract hypothetical version of your future crap together before you show up in your child's life. They need you now more than ever. It makes sense, in theory, that while you're not your usual solid self, you'd want to hide from the world and especially your kids; but stepping out at such a crucial time only adds to the insecurity and causes damage that can sometimes be irreparable. Hiding out and letting your ex-partner take the wheel can plant the seeds of destruction that flourish for years and years to come. What you choose to do right now, and how you participate or don't participate in the lives of your children, will have massive repercussions well into their adult lives. Please don't let them be the casualty of a romantic relationship gone awry. They don't deserve that.

While going through a divorce will impact you directly, please remember it also impacts your kids. Be present, spend quality time with them and make sure that you're giving them everything they need to be successful, including good experiences that they have a say in. Do your best, and don't be afraid to bring in help and grow your support system. Just because your kids are struggling now doesn't mean they will struggle for the rest of their lives – if you take action. In the first year or two after a divorce your kids will experience a lot of emotions that you will wish you can protect them from, but ultimately all you can do is be there for them. Being there is a massive responsibility. If you can support your kids through this, and they learn important skills along the way, it gives them an early start to learning how to deal with things that most adults don't even have a clue about. Kids are resilient by nature and can bounce back and get used to all the changes in time.

I often say my kids saved my life and I honestly believe they did. As I went through my divorce, keeping them front and center was a powerful motivation for me to keep going and striving for better. I'm proud of how my ex and I dealt with our situation. We did the best we could, working together to focus on the kids and not our own crap, to ensure we minimized the impact on them. Was it easy? No. It was harder than I ever could've imagined as we put our differences aside to help raise the best kids we could. It took what felt like a superhuman amount of mental strength and willpower. But when I look at the strong, confident individuals my kids are now, I know we did some things right and you can too.

CHAPTER SIX:
WHERE THE RUBBER
MEETS THE ROAD

"The future depends on what you do today." —*Mahatma Gandhi*

If reading this book is all you do, your outlook on life may change for a few days, maybe even a few weeks. However, within a short space of time you'll quickly fall back into your old ways and the mindset you were in when you initially felt the need to pick up this book. Please know this and let it sink in – you must consistently be taking action if you want your life to change. By taking action every single day, slowly but surely these actions will begin to add up and you'll start to see changes in all aspects of your life. As you continue to build on that momentum day in and day out, your life will start to take off and the dreams you once had will start to turn into your reality.

Let's be honest; for most, change is hard. The majority of men that I have spoken to have found it downright difficult. Most actually find it easy for the first few days, maybe even weeks, however something always happens which knocks them off their path.

Your mindset, your energy levels, and your environment play a big part in setting you up for success when you start putting all of this together. In this chapter, I will share with you some strategies to ensure that when the rubber meets the road, it stays on the road; strategies that I have found to be the most effective at preparing you for what lies ahead and keeping you on track to create and achieve the future you!

Conditions Are Never Perfect

There is a great quote by Tim Ferriss in his book The 4-Hour Workweek: "For all of the most important things, the timing always sucks. Waiting for a good time to quit your job? The stars will never align, and the traffic lights of life will never all be green at the same time. The universe doesn't conspire against you, but it doesn't go out of its way to line up the pins either. Conditions are never perfect. "Someday" is a disease that will take your dreams to the grave with you. Pro and con lists are just as bad. If it's important to you and you want to do it "eventually," just do it and correct course along the way".

There is usually never a good time to start something. Waiting for the perfect moment will end in delay and disappointment. The secret is simple: you just have to start, and what better time than now? Today is the day to make yourself a promise that from this day forward, you will commit to doing anything and everything to design, create, and move forward towards the new you and your new life, no matter what life throws at you. Any challenge that comes across your path will be a gift; one that will allow you to grow, and make you stronger in more ways than you can imagine. Remember, Rome was not built in a day, and neither will the new YOU be. It takes time. Be patient with the process but stay committed to the end goal. Please, start today and begin to put everything in this book into practice. You'll thank me and your future self for it.

Now, if you find yourself wandering off your path, that's OK! At least you recognized that you veered off before you got totally lost. Give yourself a high five! At this point, I would stop and ask yourself what caused you to wander off and then when you understand why, address it so that it doesn't happen again. Here's a little story that I'll use as an example: A few months after Vlad and his girlfriend split up, he was going to the gym five to six days a week and he was feeling great. After switching jobs, he started to hang out with his new teammates after work and they often went to the pub for a drink to talk about their day. It didn't take him long to realize that he had fallen of the path of putting his health first. In his words, "I got distracted". Once he had realized this, he chose to go back to honouring his commitment to health, and suggested to his team they go with him to the gym as most were not in the best of health. Guess what? They did, and it turned into a gift not just for Vlad, but for his is teammates too.

Overthinking is Bad for Your Health

The classic definition of overthinking is to think about something too much or for too long. That doesn't sound that harmful, right? Wrong! While it's human nature to think things through when making a decision or evaluating a given situation, overthinking happens when you can't get out of your own head and make a decision on something. It causes you to become paralyzed instead of taking action and moving forward with life. This is also known as "paralysis by analysis".

So why do we overthink? In short, it's because we're afraid to do the wrong thing so we get caught in a loop of think and re-think, leading to no decision making and no taking action – which causes us to think about it even more! Overthinking is detrimental in that it can increase depression, elevate your stress levels, and cloud your judgment – hence the reason it's bad for your health! So how do you break the circuit of overthinking?

The first step is to recognize the "story you're telling yourself". Remember in Chapter 2: Emotional Mastery, we spoke about "stop believing in scary tales"? The story that you're telling yourself, which you believe in that moment to be true, is the basis of what's holding you back from making a decision to move forward. As you continue to overthink, the fictitious story will shapeshift as you come up with new thoughts, ideas, or ways of dealing with a given situation or person. If you look deep enough, you might even find that crafty ego hanging around chiming in on the story too. The question is, does the story you're telling yourself empower you, or hold you back? You need to change the story line to one that empowers you to take action and move your life forward. You also need to welcome any emotions that are present and ask them why they are there. This will give you some powerful insight into why you are overthinking. Remember, you are not your emotions!

The second step is to take some form of immediate action towards the issue or situation you are overthinking. It does not have to be a big action; it could be something as small as sending a text, booking an appointment online, buying that book, going to the shopping mall, sending an email asking for more information, scheduling time in your calendar to do something or brainstorming an idea in your journal. The point here is not to leave the scene of overthinking without taking an action. It's the best way to short-circuit the process and train your mind for future overthinking episodes. As you begin to master "taking action", you will naturally go to that state instead of overthinking.

If You Fail to Plan, Then You're Planning to Fail

Benjamin Franklin once said, "If you fail to plan, you are planning to fail." I don't believe anyone sets out planning to fail, but excuses like too many priorities, not enough time, or having a lack of self-discipline, results in our failure to plan which in turn results in the huge difference between moving towards the life you want, and staying stuck with a life you don't. Please understand this!

Planning is actually straightforward. In most cases, you already know what you need to do; so you have two choices: first – do it now in this moment, or secondly – take out whatever calendar system you use to plan your life, and book it in. Please don't overthink this, just do it. If you're not clear about what it is you specifically need to do, grab a pen and paper, and start brainstorming all the things or steps you need to take to achieve the thing that you want to get done. Then decide what actions need to be done first and schedule them immediately.

My favourite acronym for PLAN is "Please Layout Actions Now!" Here is an example of how you can take your Future Map that you created in Chapter 4: Your Future You, and use that as the basis for taking action.

Take out your Future Map and pick one of the following key areas of life that you went into detail on (ideally you want to pick the one that needs the most amount of work):

- Health & Fitness
- Mind & Emotions
- Family & Friends
- Money & Finances
- Fun & Experiences
- Career & Business
- Growth & Development
- Relationships & Love

Now that you have the key area you want to focus on, look inside that area and pick one thing that you'd like to work on. For example, let's say you picked Family & Friends, and inside that you want to focus on the goal of meeting new friends. You can now brainstorm this further and make a list of places you could go, or groups you could join, to meet new people. Now let's take this one step further. Pick one thing you wrote down; let's say it was to attend a network meeting. Now! research the network meetings that are going on around your area. Once you have found one, you have two choices; book and confirm your attendance if that option is available, or schedule some time in your calendar to call the organizer in the next few days to sign up. Simple, right? Now do that for any area of your life in which you need to move forward.

Taking the time to plan will exponentially increase the chance of you moving towards the life you want. Please, don't leave things to the last minute or up to chance to sort themselves out. Success doesn't happen by accident. You make it happen!

Focus on What You Can Control

It is totally pointless to try to change things you cannot control, so why try? I personally think the reason people do this is because it gives them an "out" of taking responsibility for their life when things don't go the way they want them to. When you want someone or something else to change and it doesn't, then you have a reason – an excuse – to tell everyone that it's someone else's problem and not yours. If you focus on something that is in your control and it doesn't work out, then that's all on you my friend! And if you struggle with that, then please re-read Chapter 1 to remind yourself of the power of taking accountability for your life.

The rule here is simple: when you are making choices around which actions you need to take to move your life forward in any area, make sure those actions are ones that are within your control. If they are not in your control, ask yourself "what action can I take to ensure this happens?", and do that action instead.

Taking action does not guarantee you success. What it does guarantee is that you are moving your life forward. In the end, your actions may not generate the results you want, and that's OK. You'll learn something from it, and then you can decide to change your strategy moving forward. Remember, life happens for you, not to you. The lessons you learn along the way are gifts; however, they are only gifts if you look at them through that lens.

Environmental Controls

You may not even realize it, but your environment shapes who you are and how you feel in surprising ways. Your environment can include your neighborhood, the house or apartment you live in, your friends and family, people you hang out with, where you work, how you commute every day, the hobbies you have, the food you consume, how much you drink, what you read and watch, how much social media content you consume – you get the picture. All of this has an incredible impact on your motivation and energy levels, and if they are not aligned with the future you want, then you'll be out of alignment with where you want to go.

One of your most important environments is the space in which you reside; the physical place you live in. It could be your matrimonial home that your ex has moved out of, an apartment or house you are renting, or a friend's place you're staying in. It's important to set up that space in such a way that allows you to heal and move on. For example, if you are living in your matrimonial home, make sure you change it up and make it yours. Put some pictures up that motivate you, change the colours of the walls, move the furniture around – do what feels good for you. Keeping the place the same as when you and your ex lived there, with wedding pictures still hanging and memories of your life together scattered around the house, will not support your healing journey. Constant reminders of your relationship all around you is not a good emotional environment to live in.

Another environment that doesn't come up a lot but is equally important are your friends or those you hang around with. If you remember in Chapter 3, we talked about building your A-Team. It's vital that you surround yourself with individuals who are just as committed to your happiness and health as you are. These individuals will play an important role in positively supporting you on your journey. Don't underestimate the power of those you spend time with. There is a great quote from the late Jim Rohn that sums this up – "you are the average of the five people you spend the most time with". I suggest you give that a lot of thought.

Attitude of Gratitude

Gratitude is a powerful antidote for many things; however, it does one thing that I consider to be a life saver – it brings you back to the present moment, snapping you out of the funk you may be in, and reminds you of the things that truly matter to you. Whenever I found myself lost in negative or emotional thoughts, or if I was having a really bad day, I would take out my journal and write down everything that I was grateful for and eventually the stress, worry, and anxiety melted away leaving me feeling aware and grateful for the abundance of great things in my world.

When you create a daily habit of having an attitude of gratitude, you build that muscle of truly being appreciative of everything in life. To begin, write down five things that you are grateful for when you wake up, and again just before going to sleep so that it's the last thing you think about before your head hits that pillow. Doing this regularly will create a conscious habit of being thankful and appreciative for every part of your life. Having an attitude of gratitude means you operate from a place of abundance rather than scarcity, which will leave you feeling happier and generally more positive.

Summary and Closing

The conditions for taking action when building your new life will never be perfect. If you wait for the stars to align perfectly, you will be waiting a long time before you do anything. The best time to take action is today and please don't over think it. I implore you to start taking action today and take the first step towards building the life that you want.

Planning is foundational when taking action. You need to have a plan in place to keep you on track. Remember, if you fail to plan, then you're planning to fail

Please don't underestimate how important your environment is to your success. Where you live, the friends you hang around with, your family, the habits you have etc. These will either support you in achieving the life you want, or they will hold you back. Take notice of your environment, and change it up where you need to.

And finally, create and maintain an attitude of gratitude. Life is not always bad, I promise you. If you look hard enough, there will always be plenty of things to be grateful for. Gratitude is a powerful way of grounding you in the present; it's magical power will remind you of all the amazing things you have in your life no matter how big or small.

Congratulations on making it to the end of this book! Your dedication and commitment to designing and living a life you want is clear. I honour you for that.

Please don't waste this opportunity. After putting everything you have learnt in this book into practice, you will now have all the tools you need to design and live the life you want. Remember, no one said this work is easy. It's not. You picked this book up for a reason. You had a choice of continuing to live a life that was going in the wrong direction, but you decided to go down a different path;

a path that you get to influence, create, enjoy and be proud of.

As you embark on your journey, stay focused, stay strong, and above all, stay committed. As Viktor Frankl once said, "the meaning of life is to give life meaning".

You have your whole life ahead of you.

Start living it NOW!

Made in the USA
Las Vegas, NV
09 March 2024

86942592R00069